Adult Literacy
core curriculum

including Spoken Communication

Acknowledgements

The Basic Skills Agency would like to thank the following for their contribution to the development of the Core Curriculum:

Martin Good, *Cambridge Training and Development Ltd.*

Freda Hollin, *Cambridge Training and Development Ltd.*

Angela Simpson, *Education Consultant*

Andrew Steeds, *Consultant and Editor*

Heather Clary, *Consultant*

Sue Henderson, *Birmingham Core Skills Partnership*

Norma Yates, *Birmingham Core Skills Partnership*

Trish Cavalot, *Birmingham Core Skills Partnership*

Nicky Thorpe, *Birmingham Core Skills Partnership*

Mark Houlton, *Consultant*

Karen Davies, *Business and Education Consultancy*

Madeleine Held, *London Language and Literacy Unit*

Helen Sunderland, *London Language and Literacy Unit*

and from the Basic Skills Agency:

Jim Pateman

Gay Lobley

Sarah Blackmore.

The Basic Skills Agency would also like to thank those organisations and individuals who responded to the consultation on the draft curriculum and, in particular, the Further Education Development Agency (FEDA) and the Qualifications and Curriculum Authority (QCA) for their detailed responses.

Produced by Cambridge Training and Development Ltd. on behalf of the Basic Skills Agency, Commonwealth House, 1–19 New Oxford Street, London WC1A 1NU.

Design: Studio 21

Editor: Andrew Steeds

ISBN 1-85990-127-1

The Agency would also like to thank the following for permission to reproduce materials in the Basic Skills Core Curriculum: The Home Office, page 69; Hodder and Stoughton, page 78; Société des Produits Nestlé S.A., pages 98–100.

Contents

Foreword

Improving the nation's literacy and numeracy skills is one of the Government's top priorities. We have already brought about significant improvements at school level and want to ensure that adults have good opportunities to develop their skills too. We are in the process of introducing a range of new measures to help them.

One of our first tasks is to improve the quality and consistency of provision. This new adult literacy and numeracy curriculum, based on the national standards developed by the Qualifications and Curriculum Authority, will be central to achieving that goal.

It provides teachers with a comprehensive framework to help identify and meet each person's individual learning needs, including examples of teaching strategies they can use. For learners, it will ensure that, no matter which type of course they choose or where the learning takes place, they can be confident of a common approach and effective support.

I am sure that this curriculum will prove an invaluable tool. It is designed primarily for adult literacy and numeracy teachers and tutors, but it will also be highly useful to programme managers, developers of literacy and numeracy training and materials, and to the growing body of organisations and individuals involved in addressing adult literacy and numeracy issues.

Malcolm Wicks MP,
Minister for Lifelong Learning

Introduction

A national strategy to tackle the literacy and numeracy needs of adults was launched by the government in the Autumn of 2000. Following the report of Sir Claus Moser's Working Group, *A Fresh Start – Improving Literacy and Numeracy* (DfEE, 1999), the government committed itself, the education services and a cross-section of agencies and national bodies to a major reduction in the number of adults who struggle with basic reading, writing, spelling and maths.

The strategy includes national standards of adult literacy and numeracy to ensure consistency, a core curriculum to clarify what teachers should teach to enable learners to reach those standards, a new system of qualifications to measure achievement against the standards, and improved quality and diversity of learning opportunities to meet the needs of a wide range of learners. This strategy sets a challenge to us all.

The adult literacy and numeracy core curriculum

The new adult literacy and numeracy core curriculum is central to the national strategy. It sets out the entitlement to learning for all adults who have difficulties with literacy and numeracy. It describes the content of what should be taught in literacy and numeracy programmes in: further and adult education; the workplace and programmes for the unemployed; prisons; community-based and family literacy and numeracy programmes. It assists teachers to meet the individual needs of adults through the selection and teaching of skills appropriate to those adults' needs. For the first time, adults and the teachers who work with them have a clear set of skills required to meet national standards, together with the knowledge and understanding that underpin those skills, supported by sample strategies to develop them.

> 'One of the crucial elements of the proposed strategy must be clarity about the skills, knowledge and understanding that anyone needs to be literate and numerate in the modern world. These skills need to be enshrined in a new curriculum, with well-developed and understood standards.'
>
> Chapter 10 (A New Basic Skills Curriculum and a New System of Qualifications), *A Fresh Start*, February 1999

The core curriculum has been written primarily for use by adult literacy and numeracy teachers and tutors. However, it will be an important document for programme managers and developers, for those involved in research and for a wider group of those bodies and individuals that are increasingly concerned with the adult literacy and numeracy agenda.

The core curriculum is based on the national standards for adult literacy and numeracy developed by the Qualifications and Curriculum Authority (QCA) in 2000. Its publication follows national consultation with teachers and managers of adult literacy and numeracy programmes, and relevant national bodies. The core curriculum draws heavily on existing and planned curricula and strategies in this country and overseas, specifically:

- the twin frameworks for teaching literacy and numeracy that are elaborated in the National Literacy Strategy and the National Numeracy Strategy;
- the new key skills units in communication and application of number developed by QCA;
- the revised National Curriculum for English and mathematics introduced in schools in September 2000;

- adult literacy and numeracy curricula and initiatives that have been developed in other countries (and, in particular, in the United States of America, Australia, Canada and France).

As the national strategy unfolds, the core curriculum will be reviewed and updated to build in new and revised ways of delivering these skills in order to fulfil the vision outlined in *A Fresh Start*. For teachers, therefore, the new core curriculum is both a key support and also a challenge.

Adult literacy and numeracy teachers will be able to use the core curriculum to develop learning programmes. It will help them to:

- use information from diagnostic assessment to identify learners' skills, both those that they already have and those that they need;

- draw those elements from the curriculum into the learning plan and assessment regime;

- use their knowledge of the learners' context and priorities to find relevant applications where learners can practise the skills and knowledge they are acquiring;

- follow the progression through the standards and the curriculum elements to build a formative and summative assessment regime into the learning plan.

Inclusivity and access

The adult literacy and numeracy core curriculum shares the basic principles of inclusivity and access that are laid down in the National Curriculum for schools:

Education is . . . a route to equality of opportunity for all, a healthy and just democracy, a productive economy, and sustainable development. Education should reflect the enduring values that contribute to these ends. These include valuing ourselves, our families and other relationships, the wider groups to which we belong, the diversity in our society and the environment in which we live.

. . . (Education) must enable us to respond positively to the opportunities and challenges of the rapidly changing world in which we live and work. In particular, we need to be prepared to engage as individuals, parents, workers and citizens with economic, social and cultural change, including the continued globalisation of the economy and society, with new work and leisure patterns and with the rapid expansion of communication technologies.

The . . . Curriculum secures . . . for all, irrespective of social background, culture, race, gender, differences in ability and disabilities, an entitlement to a number of areas of learning and to develop knowledge, understanding, skills and attitudes necessary for their self-fulfilment and development as active and responsible citizens.

('The school curriculum and the National Curriculum: values, aims and purposes', *The National Curriculum*, DfEE, 1999)

Some adults will have special requirements. The following access statement applies to the standards at each level:

Adults with a disability may have special learning requirements and be unable to demonstrate some of the capabilities or skills specified in the standards. As a reasonable adjustment and to aid access it is recommended that alternative methods are investigated to allow individual to demonstrate their abilities.

Curriculum developers and qualifications designers are expected to produce guidance for centres on recognising special learning requirements. This guidance should be supported by a framework for identifying and adopting appropriate alternative approaches.

('Access to the standards', *National standards for adult literacy and numeracy*, QCA, 2000)

Guidance on specialist diagnosis of learning needs and access to the curriculum for learners with physical disabilities, sensory impairment and learning disabilities will be published separately.

The national standards for adult literacy and numeracy

The standards describe adult literacy and numeracy within the definition expressed in *A Fresh Start*:

'the ability to read, write and speak in English and to use mathematics at a level necessary to function at work and in society in general.'

The standards provide a map of the range of skills and capabilities that adults are expected to need in order to function and progress at work and in society. A separate set of standards has been produced for each of the basic skills of literacy and numeracy.

Literacy covers the ability to:

- speak, listen and respond
- read and comprehend
- write to communicate.

Numeracy covers the ability to:

- understand and use mathematical information
- calculate and manipulate mathematical information
- interpret results and communicate mathematical information.

Separate curricula have been developed and published for literacy and for numeracy.

The national qualifications framework

The national standards for adult literacy and numeracy are specified at three levels: Entry level, Level 1 and Level 2. Levels 1 and 2 are aligned to the key skills of communication and application of number (this alignment is signposted on the left-hand page of the curriculum document at these levels). Entry level is further divided into three sub-levels: Entry 1, Entry 2 and Entry 3. Entry level has been set out in this way to describe in detail the small steps required for adults to make progress. This sub-division also signals a clear alignment of the skill levels with levels 1, 2 and 3 of the National Curriculum.

The three levels of the national standards for adult literacy and numeracy correspond to the levels of demand of qualifications in the national qualifications framework, illustrated in Table 1.

Table 1. The national qualifications framework

National Curriculum	Literacy/Numeracy	Key skills	National qualifications framework
		Key skills Level 5	National qualifications framework Level 5
		Key skills Level 4	National qualifications framework Level 4
		Key skills Level 3	National qualifications framework Level 3
	Literacy/Numeracy Level 2	Key skills Level 2	National qualifications framework Level 2
National Curriculum Level 5	Literacy/Numeracy Level 1	Key skills Level 1	National qualifications framework Level 1
National Curriculum Level 4			
National Curriculum Level 3	Literacy/Numeracy Entry 3		
National Curriculum Level 2	Literacy/Numeracy Entry 2		Entry Level
National Curriculum Level 1	Literacy/Numeracy Entry 1		

Who are the learners?

Over 7 million adults in England have difficulties with literacy and numeracy. This means that they are unable to read and write very well and have difficulty doing some of the simplest tasks such as writing a letter, reading a piece of text or calculating change – tasks that most of us take for granted.

But we know that the 7 million adults struggling with literacy and numeracy are not a homogeneous group. They're 7 million individuals with different needs, attitudes and interests. We also know that they don't all have the same degree of difficulties with literacy and numeracy.

Research by the Basic Skills Agency has identified three attainment groups that make up the 7 million:

- a higher-level group (just over 4 million adults) who need fairly modest help to 'brush up' their skills to the required level;
- a middle-level group (just under 1.5 million adults) who have greater difficulty and need more specific and in-depth help;
- a lower-level group (just under 1.5 million adults) who require intensive teaching by specialist teachers.

In addition, there are an estimated 500,000 adults for whom English is an additional language. A separate but related curriculum has been developed for this group of learners.

Many of those with low levels of literacy and numeracy are working. For example, recent research showed that, among the 7 million adults with very low or low literacy, the following proportions were employed:

- 57 per cent of men in their twenties
- 72 per cent of men in their thirties
- 74 per cent of women in their forties.[1]

However, we know that low levels of literacy and numeracy limit the employment opportunities available to individuals. A 1993 survey found that:

- people without any Entry level skills had access to only one in 50 of lower level jobs;
- those with Entry level skills had access to 50 per cent;
- those with Level 1 skills had access to 75 per cent.[2]

As jobs continue to change, and new technological, quality and work organisation systems are introduced, this situation is likely to get worse.

---

1. *Literacy, Leaving School and Jobs: the effect of poor basic skills on employment in different age groups,* The Basic Skills Agency, 1999
2. *Basic Skills and Jobs,* Institute for Employment Studies, 1993

Using the adult literacy core curriculum

The new adult literacy core curriculum is organised across double pages as follows:

National standard

Each standard for speaking and listening, reading and writing is listed in the adult literacy core curriculum. A summary page showing progression between capabilities at each level is included on pages 10–11.

Curriculum element

The adult literacy core curriculum is broken down into the skills and knowledge required to meet each standard. The curriculum elements are made up of the **descriptors** (the term given to skills listed underneath each standard at each level in the national standards for adult literacy and numeracy published by QCA) for each standard, as well as **additional skills and knowledge** necessary for the achievement of the standard. Descriptors are shown in bold; additional skills and knowledge are in a lighter typeface.

(At Levels 1 and 2 the curriculum's alignment to the key skills of communication is given on the left-hand page.)

Example

An example of a relevant literacy task is attached to each of the curriculum elements. The examples are not intended to define or prescribe tasks, but to make the demands of the level clear.

Sample activities

The right-hand pages list sample activities that can be used to develop the skills and knowledge related to each curriculum element.

Guidance

The right-hand pages also contain guidance on techniques and approaches that teachers will use to develop literacy.

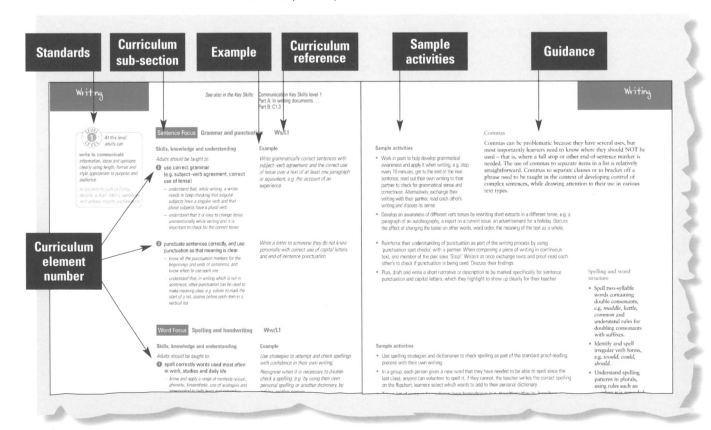

Curriculum referencing

To assist teachers in their planning, the adult literacy core curriculum uses a reference system (indicated on the sample double page on the previous page) that breaks the core curriculum into its component parts of: curriculum section, curriculum sub-section, level and curriculum element. Pages 12–19 uses this reference system to provide a detailed account of the progression between curriculum elements across the levels.

Key to reference system

Curriculum sections and sub-sections

Speaking and Listening	SL	Reading	R	Writing	W
Listen and respond	SLlr	Text	Rt	Text	Wt
Speak to communicate	SLc	Sentence	Rs	Sentence	Ws
Engage in discussion	SLd	Word	Rw	Word	Ww

The adult literacy core curriculum makes clear the links between the standards and the teaching and learning of the skills, knowledge and understanding required to meet the standards. However, in the teaching context, on many occasions, activities are likely to be integrated in order to address different standards at the same time. For example, a discussion simultaneously:

- might be developing skills to meet the standards for listening, speaking and discussion;
- might be based on a topic which learners have researched previously through reading;
- may form preparation for writing at some point.

Glossary

The adult literacy core curriculum contains a glossary of terms used, which draws on the glossary developed for the National Literacy Strategy in schools. The glossary also includes qualifying terms such as *straightforward* and *everyday*.

Text, sentence and word focus

The adult literacy core curriculum uses a model of literacy that differentiates between three dimensions in the processes of reading and writing. This model, which forms a central part of the National Literacy Strategy in schools, recognises the complexity of the reading process, and the different levels on which fluent readers operate:

- **text focus** addresses the overall meaning of the text, the ability to read critically and flexibly and write in different styles and forms
- **sentence focus** deals with grammar and sentence structure
- **word focus** looks at the individual words themselves, their structure, spelling and individual character.

The model makes the elements involved in developing literacy skills more explicit. However, it is not intended that these three dimensions should be taught one after the other; teachers will draw simultaneously on all three in their work on reading and writing. This reflects the mix of skills that fluent readers need to use when they read something new. They use their knowledge of text to work out what kind of reading they need to do; they use sentence-focus skills to understand the text; and they use word-focus skills to work out any words they are not familiar with.

It is critical that the adult literacy core curriculum is used in this integrated way. It is not a list of separate and discrete activities. Text-, sentence- and word-focus elements must all be covered, and the core curriculum includes activities which focus on specific skills; however, in many cases, teaching and learning activities will cover more than one aspect.

To illustrate in more detail how text-, sentence- and word-focus work inter-relate, at each level there is an example of an integrated activity built around a text. These can be found at the end of each level of the reading curriculum. They aim to show how learners can be taught to apply a range of reading strategies – on the whole text, on sentences and on individual words – from the earliest stages, to help them read with understanding. As learners progress, the extent and sophistication of their strategies increase, and they can apply them to more complicated texts.

In the process of reading texts in this way, adults extend their knowledge and experience of the characteristics of different types of writing, at text, sentence and word level. They can then apply this understanding to their own writing, and use their increasing knowledge of how written texts work to extend their own repertoire and range of writing skills. Thus integrated reading activities can also be used as a way into talking about writing at text, sentence and word level in preparation for learners doing their own writing.

The integrated activities, like most activities throughout the adult literacy core curriculum, involve speaking, listening and discussion. In the process of developing their reading and writing skills, adults must talk together, e.g. to complete tasks, to understand specific features, to extend their understanding of processes, concepts and ideas.

As well as the inter-relationship between text-, sentence- and word-level work and between reading, writing and spoken communication on which the integrated activities are based, specific links are signalled at the end of each activity. These illustrate the sorts of writing task and spoken communication activity that might arise from work on these particular texts.

Reading and writing – separately or together?

Although the National Literacy Strategy sets out reading and writing in parallel, they are separated in the adult literacy core curriculum. It is very common for adults with literacy problems to be at a higher level in reading than they are in writing. Some of the component skills and knowledge in reading and writing are also distinct, even though closely related to each other.

Similarly, while speaking, listening and discussion are skills in their own right of fundamental importance in work and social life, they are also an essential aspect of improving reading and writing skills. Adults who talk and listen with their tutor and other learners as part of the process of developing their reading and writing skills are much more likely to recognise the relationship of parts to the whole, to grasp some underlying principles and to reflect on their development as readers and writers.

The learner's context

If the adult literacy core curriculum is to be successful, it is important that:

- the learner is clear about what they are learning and what the activities they are undertaking are designed to teach – a clear and consistently delivered curriculum helps with this;

- the learner brings the context that will be the ultimate 'proving' ground for their improved skills;

- the learner is sure that the skills and knowledge that they are learning are helping them to use their literacy in the range of ways they want.

The curriculum elements must be clear and used *with* learners. The aim must be that they develop the concepts and the language that will help them make sense of their learning and go on doing it. Evidence shows that the inclusion of explicit curriculum targets in learning programmes has resulted in a clearer identification of outcomes **by learners** as well as by teachers, and in better attendance and progression by learners.

The skills and knowledge elements in the adult literacy core curriculum are generic. They are the basic building blocks that everyone needs in order to use literacy skills effectively in everyday life. What is different is how adults use these skills and the widely differing past experiences that they bring to their learning. This is the *context* that the learner provides. Each individual learner will come with their own set of priorities and requirements, and these must be the starting point of their learning programme development.

The section in the national standards on the 'Structure of the standards' provides examples of the use of literacy and numeracy skills in different contexts under the following headings:

- citizen and community
- economic activity, including paid and unpaid work
- domestic and everyday life
- leisure
- education and training
- using ICT in social roles.

These are examples of the social roles and activities in which adults need literacy and numeracy in order to function independently and exercise choice. This adult literacy core curriculum provides the skills framework, the learner provides the context, and the tutor needs to bring them together in a learning programme using relevant materials at the appropriate level, to support learners in achieving their goals.

> 'Learners should be able to develop the skills common to them all, using the interests, the materials and the activities that most closely match their needs'
> *A Fresh Start*

> 'In short, the curriculum is not a series of rigid lesson plans to be taught by every teacher and followed by every learner'.
> *A Fresh Start*

The progression between capabilities

Entry Level		

ENTRY 1	**ENTRY 2**	**ENTRY 3**
Speaking and listening *At this level, adults can*	*Speaking and listening* *At this level, adults can*	*Speaking and listening* *At this level, adults can*
listen and respond to spoken language, including simple narratives, statements, questions and single-step instructions	listen and respond to spoken language, including straightforward information, short narratives, explanations and instructions	listen and respond to spoken language, including straightforward information and narratives, and follow straightforward explanations and instructions, both face to face and on the telephone
speak to communicate basic information, feelings and opinions on familiar topics	speak to communicate information, feelings and opinions on familiar topics	speak to communicate information, feelings and opinions on familiar topics, using appropriate formality, both face to face and on the telephone
engage in discussion with another person in a familiar situation about familiar topics	engage in discussion with one or more people in a familiar situation to establish shared understanding about familiar topics	engage in discussion with one or more people in a familiar situation, making relevant points and responding to what others say to reach a shared understanding about familiar topics
Reading *At this level, adults can*	*Reading* *At this level, adults can*	*Reading* *At this level, adults can*
read and understand short texts with repeated language patterns on familiar topics	read and understand short, straightforward texts on familiar topics	read and understand short, straightforward texts on familiar topics accurately and independently
read and obtain information from common signs and symbols	read and obtain information from short documents, familiar sources and signs and symbols	read and obtain information from everyday sources
Writing *At this level, adults can*	*Writing* *At this level, adults can*	*Writing* *At this level, adults can*
write to communicate information to an intended audience	write to communicate information with some awareness of the intended audience	write to communicate information and opinions with some adaptation to the intended audience

LEVEL 1	**LEVEL 2**
Speaking and listening *At this level, adults can*	*Speaking and listening* *At this level, adults can*
listen and respond to spoken language, including information and narratives, and follow explanations and instructions of varying lengths, adapting response to speaker, medium and context	**listen and respond** to spoken language, including extended information and narratives, and follow detailed explanations and multi-step instructions of varying length, adapting response to speaker, medium and context
speak to communicate information, ideas and opinions adapting speech and content to take account of the listener(s) and medium	**speak to communicate** straightforward and detailed information, ideas and opinions clearly, adapting speech and content to take account of the listener(s), medium, purpose and situation
engage in discussion with one or more people in familiar and unfamiliar situations, making clear and relevant contributions that respond to what others say and produce a shared understanding about different topics	**engage in discussion** with one or more people in a variety of different situations, making clear and effective contributions that produce outcomes appropriate to purpose and topic
Reading *At this level, adults can*	*Reading* *At this level, adults can*
read and understand straightforward texts of varying length on a variety of topics accurately and independently	**read and understand** a range of texts of varying complexity accurately and independently
read and obtain information from different sources	**read and obtain information** of varying length and detail from different sources
Writing *At this level, adults can*	*Writing* *At this level, adults can*
write to communicate information, ideas and opinions clearly using length, format and style appropriate to purpose and audience	**write to communicate** information, ideas and opinions clearly and effectively, using length, format and style appropriate to purpose, content and audience

Speaking and listening: the progression between curriculum elements

	Entry Level	
	ENTRY 1 LEVEL	**ENTRY 2 LEVEL**
Listen and respond	**SLlr/E1.1** Listen for the gist of short explanations **SLlr/E1.2** Listen for detail using key words to extract some specific information **SLlr/E1.3** Follow single-step instructions in a familiar context, asking for instructions to be repeated if necessary **SLlr/E1.4** Listen and respond to requests for personal information	**SLlr/E2.1** Listen for and follow the gist of explanations, instructions and narratives **SLlr/E2.2** Listen for detail in short explanations, instructions and narratives **SLlr/E2.3** Listen for and identify the main points of short explanations or presentations **SLlr/E2.4** Listen to and follow short, straightforward explanations and instructions **SLlr/E2.5** Listen to and identify simply expressed feelings and opinions **SLlr/E2.6** Respond to straightforward questions
Speak to communicate	**SLc/E1.1** Speak clearly to be heard and understood in simple exchanges **SLc/E1.2** Make requests using appropriate terms **SLc/E1.3** Ask questions to obtain specific information **SLc/E1.4** Make statements of fact clearly	**SLc/E2.1** Speak clearly to be heard and understood in straightforward exchanges **SLc/E2.2** Make requests and ask questions to obtain information in everyday contexts **SLc/E2.3** Express clearly statements of fact, and short accounts and descriptions **SLc/E2.4** Ask questions to clarify understanding
Engage in discussion	**SLd/E1.1** Speak and listen in simple exchanges and everyday contexts	**SLc/E2.1** Follow the gist of discussions **SLc/E2.2** Follow the main points and make appropriate contributions to the discussion

ENTRY LEVEL 3	LEVEL 1	LEVEL 2
SLlr/E3.1 Listen for and follow the gist of explanations, instructions and narratives in different contexts **SLlr/E3.2** Listen for detail in explanations, instructions and narratives in different contexts **SLlr/E3.3** Listen for and identify relevant information and new information from discussions, explanations and presentations **SLlr/E3.4** Use strategies to clarify and confirm understanding (e.g. facial expressions or gestures) **SLlr/E3.5** Listen to and respond appropriately to other points of view **SLlr/E3.6** Respond to a range of questions about familiar topics	**SLlr/L1.1** Listen for and identify relevant information from explanations and presentations on a range of straightforward topics **SLlr/L1.2** Listen for and understand explanations, instructions and narratives on different topics in a range of contexts **SLlr/L1.3** Use strategies to clarify and confirm understanding (e.g. facial expressions, body language and verbal prompts) **SLlr/L1.4** Provide feedback and confirmation when listening to others **SLlr/L1.5** Make contributions relevant to the situation and the subject **SLlr/L1.6** Respond to questions on a range of topics	**SLlr/L2.1** Listen for and identify relevant information from extended explanations or presentations on a range of topics **SLlr/L2.2** Listen to, understand and follow lengthy or multi-step instructions and narratives on a range of topics and in a range of contexts **SLlr/L2.3** Respond to detailed or extended questions on a range of topics **SLlr/L2.4** Respond to criticism and criticise constructively
SLc/E3.1 Speak clearly to be heard and understood using appropriate clarity, speed and phrasing **SLc/E3.2** Use formal language and register when appropriate **SLc/E3.3** Express clearly statements of fact and give short explanations, accounts and descriptions **SLc/E3.4** Make requests and ask questions to obtain information in familiar and unfamiliar contexts	**SLc/L1.1** Speak clearly in a way which suits the situation **SLc/L1.2** Make requests and ask questions to obtain information in familiar and unfamiliar contexts **SLc/L1.3** Express clearly statements of fact, explanations, instructions, accounts, and descriptions **SLc/L1.4** Present information and ideas in a logical sequence and include detail and develop ideas where appropriate	**SLc/L2.1** Speak clearly and confidently in a way which suits the situation **SLc/L2.2** Make requests and ask questions to obtain detailed information in familiar and unfamiliar contexts **SLc/L2.3** Express clearly statements of fact, explanations, instructions, accounts, descriptions using appropriate structure, style and vocabulary **SLc/L2.4** Present information and ideas in a logical sequence and provide further detail and development to clarify or confirm understanding
SLd/E3.1 Follow and understand the main points of discussions on different topics **SLd/E3.2** Make contributions to discussions that are relevant to the subject **SLd/E3.3** Respect the turn-taking rights of others during discussions	**SLd/L1.1** Follow and contribute to discussions on a range of straightforward topics **SLd/L1.2** Respect the turn-taking rights of others during discussions **SLd/L1.3** Use appropriate phrases for interruption	**SLd/L2.1** Make relevant contributions and help to move discussions forward **SLd/L2.2** Adapt contributions to discussions to suit audience, context, purpose and situation **SLd/L2.3** Use appropriate phrases for interruption and change of topic **SLd/L2.4** Support opinions and arguments with evidence **SLd/L2.5** Use strategies intended to reassure (e.g. body language and appropriate phraseology)

Reading and Writing (Text focus): the progression between curriculum elements

READING ☐   WRITING ☐

Entry Level		

TEXT FOCUS	ENTRY LEVEL 1	ENTRY LEVEL 2
Reading comprehension	**Rt/E1.1** Follow a short narrative on a familiar topic or experience **Rt/E1.2** Recognise the different purposes of texts at this level	**Rt/E2.1** Trace and understand the main events of chronological and instructional texts **Rt/E2.2** Recognise the different purposes of texts at this level **Rt/E2.3** Identify common sources of information **Rt/E2.4** Use illustrations and captions to locate information
Writing composition	**Wt/E1.1** Use written words and phrases to record or present information	**Wt/E2.1** Use written words and phrases to record or present information

ENTRY LEVEL 3	LEVEL 1	LEVEL 2
Rt/E3.1 Trace and understand the main events of chronological, continuous descriptive and explanatory texts of more than one paragraph **Rt/E3.2** Recognise the different purposes of texts at this level **Rt/E3.3** Recognise and understand the organisational features and typical language of instructional texts (e.g. use of imperatives and second person) **Rt/E3.4** Identify the main points and ideas, and predict words from context **Rt/E3.5** Understand and use organisational features to locate information (e.g. contents, index, menus) **Rt/E3.6** Skim read title, headings and illustrations to decide if material is of interest **Rt/E3.7** Scan texts to locate information **Rt/E3.8** Obtain specific information through detailed reading **Rt/E3.9** Relate an image to print and use it to obtain meaning	**Rt/L1.1** Trace and understand the main events of continuous descriptive, explanatory and persuasive texts **Rt/L1.2** Recognise how language and other textual features are used to achieve different purposes (e.g. to instruct, explain, describe, persuade) **Rt/L1.3** Identify the main points and specific detail, and infer meaning from images which is not explicit in the text **Rt/L1.4** Use organisational and structural features to locate information (e.g. contents, index, menus, subheadings, paragraphs) **Rt/L1.5** Use different reading strategies to find and obtain information	**Rt/L2.1** Trace and understand the main events of continuous descriptive, explanatory and persuasive texts **Rt/L2.2** Identify the purpose of a text and infer meaning which is not explicit **Rt/L2.3** Identify the main points and specific detail **Rt/L2.4** Read an argument and identify the points of view **Rt/L2.5** Read critically to evaluate information, and compare information, ideas and opinions from different sources **Rt/L2.6** Use organisational features and systems to locate texts and information **Rt/L2.7** Use different reading strategies to find and obtain information (e.g. skimming, scanning, detailed reading) **Rt/L2.8** Summarise information from longer documents
Wt/E3.1 Plan and draft writing **Wt/E3.2** Organise writing in short paragraphs **Wt/E3.3** Sequence chronological writing **Wt/E3.4** Proof-read and correct writing for grammar and spelling	**Wt/L1.1** Plan and draft writing **Wt/L1.2** Judge how much to write and the level of detail to include **Wt/L1.3** Present information in a logical sequence using paragraphs where appropriate **Wt/L1.4** Use language suitable for purpose and audience **Wt/L1.5** Use format and structure for different purposes **Wt/L1.6** Proof-read and revise writing for accuracy and meaning	**Wt/L2.1** Plan and draft writing **Wt/L2.2** Judge how much to write and the level of detail to include **Wt/L2.3** Present information and ideas in a logical or persuasive sequence, using paragraphs where appropriate **Wt/L2.4** Use format and structure to organise writing for different purposes **Wt/L2.5** Use formal and informal language appropriate to purpose and audience **Wt/L2.6** Use different styles of writing for different purposes (e.g. persuasive techniques, supporting evidence, technical vocabulary) **Wt/L2.7** Proof-read and revise writing for accuracy and meaning

Reading and Writing (Sentence focus): the progression between curriculum elements

READING ☐   WRITING ☐

Entry Level		
SENTENCE FOCUS	**ENTRY LEVEL 1**	**ENTRY LEVEL 2**
Grammar and punctuation	**Rs/E1.1** Read and recognise simple sentence structures	**Rs/E2.1** Read and understand linking words and adverbials in instructions and directions (e.g. *next, then, right* and *straight on*) **Rs/E2.2** Use knowledge of simple sentence structure and word order to help decipher unfamiliar words and predict meaning **Rs/E2.3** Apply own life experience and knowledge to check out plausible meanings of a sentence as a whole when decoding unfamiliar words **Rs/E2.4** Use punctuation and capitalisation to aid understanding
Grammar and punctuation	**Ws/E1.1** Construct a simple sentence **Ws/E1.2** Punctuate a simple sentence with a capital letter and a full stop **Ws/E1.3** Use a capital letter for personal pronoun 'I'	**Ws/E2.1** Construct simple and compound sentences, using common conjunctions to connect two clauses (e.g. *as, and, but*) **Ws/E2.2** Use adjectives **Ws/E2.3** Use punctuation correctly (e.g. capital letters, full stops and question marks) **Ws/E2.4** Use a capital letter for proper nouns

ENTRY LEVEL 3	LEVEL 1	LEVEL 2
Rs/E3.1 Recognise and understand the organisational features and typical language of instructional texts (e.g. use of imperatives, second person) **Rs/E3.2** Use implicit and explicit knowledge of different types of word (e.g. linking words [connectives], nouns, verbs, adjectives), of word order, and of possible plausible meanings, to help decode unfamiliar words and predict meaning **Rs/E3.3** Use punctuation and capitalisation to aid understanding	**Rs/L1.1** Use implicit and explicit grammatical knowledge (e.g. of different sentence forms, types of word, verb tense, word order) along with own knowledge and experience to predict meaning, try out plausible meanings, and to read and check for sense **Rs/L1.2** Use punctuation to help their understanding	**Rs/L2.1** Use implicit and explicit grammatical knowledge, alongside own knowledge and experience of context, to help follow meaning and judge the purpose of different types of text **Rs/L2.2** Use punctuation to help interpret the meaning and purpose of texts
Ws/E3.1 Write in complete sentences **Ws/E3.2** Use correct basic grammar (e.g. appropriate verb tense, subject–verb agreement) **Ws/E3.3** Use punctuation correctly (e.g. capital letters, full stops, question marks, exclamation marks)	**Ws/L1.1** Write in complete sentences **Ws/L1.2** Use correct grammar (e.g. subject–verb agreement, correct use of tense) **Ws/L1.3** Punctuate sentences correctly, and use punctuation so that meaning is clear	**Ws/L2.1** Construct complex sentences **Ws/L2.2** Use correct grammar (e.g. subject–verb agreement, correct and consistent use of tense) **Ws/L2.3** Use pronouns so that their meaning is clear **Ws/L2.4** Punctuate sentences correctly, and use punctuation accurately (e.g. commas, apostrophes, inverted commas)

Reading and Writing (Word focus): the progression between curriculum elements

READING ☐   WRITING ☐

Entry Level		

WORD FOCUS	ENTRY 1 LEVEL	ENTRY 2 LEVEL
Vocabulary, word recognition and phonics	**Rw/E1.1** Possess a limited, meaningful sight vocabulary of words, signs and symbols **Rw/E1.2** Decode simple, regular words **Rw/E1.3** Recognise the letters of the alphabet in both upper and lower case	**Rw/E2.1** Read and understand words on forms related to personal information (e.g. first name, surname, address, postcode, age, date of birth) **Rw/E2.2** Recognise high-frequency words and words with common spelling patterns **Rw/E2.3** Use phonic and graphic knowledge to decode words **Rw/E2.4** Use a simplified dictionary to find the meaning of unfamiliar words **Rw/E2.5** Use initial letters to find and sequence words in alphabetical order
Spelling and handwriting	**Ww/E1.1** Spell correctly some personal key words and familiar words **Ww/E1.2** Write the letters of the alphabet using upper and lower case **Ww/E1.3** Use basic sound–symbol association to help spelling, *as appropriate for the needs of the learner*	**Ww/E2.1** Spell correctly the majority of personal details and familiar common words **Ww/E2.2** Use their knowledge of sound–symbol relationships and phonological patterns (e.g. consonant clusters and vowel phonemes) to help work out correct spellings, *as appropriate for the needs of the learner* **Ww/E2.3** Produce legible text

ENTRY LEVEL 3	LEVEL 1	LEVEL 2
Rw/E3.1 Recognise and understand relevant specialist key words **Rw/E3.2** Read and understand words and phrases commonly used on forms **Rw/E3.3** Use a dictionary to find the meaning of unfamiliar words **Rw/E3.4** Use first- and second-place letters to find and sequence words in alphabetical order **Rw/E3.5** Use a variety of reading strategies to help decode an increasing range of unfamiliar words	**Rw/L1.1** Use reference material to find the meaning of unfamiliar words **Rw/L1.2** Recognise and understand the vocabulary associated with different types of text, using appropriate strategies to work out meaning **Rw/L1.3** Recognise and understand an increasing range of vocabulary, applying knowledge of word structure, related words, word roots, derivations, borrowings	**Rw/L2.1** Read and understand technical vocabulary **Rw/L2.2** Use reference material to find the meaning of unfamiliar words **Rw/L2.3** Recognise and understand vocabulary associated with texts of different levels of accessibility, formality, complexity and of different purpose
Ww/E3.1 Spell correctly common words and relevant key words for work and special interest **Ww/E3.2** Use their developing knowledge of sound–symbol relationships and phonological patterns to help spell a greater range of words and longer words, *as appropriate for the needs of the learner* **Ww/E3.3** Produce legible text	**Ww/L1.1** Spell correctly words used most often in work, studies and daily life **Ww/L1.2** Produce legible text	**Ww/L2.1** Spell correctly words used most often in work, studies and daily life, including familiar technical words **Ww/L2.2** Produce legible text

Speaking and listening

Speaking and listening is by far the most widespread form of communication even in the most literate person's life. In most jobs people spend much more time speaking, listening and discussing than reading or writing, so it's worth knowing something about how it all works, and using that awareness to increase confidence and effectiveness. Talk is an important medium for getting things done, but equally important is the ability to listen carefully and both act and reflect on what is heard.

Many adults will not have received explicit teaching in speaking and listening before. But they will have a lot of implicit knowledge and experience – in some cases in quite specialised fields. Improving skills in speaking and listening can be about getting better at what you do, and also learning to extend what you do to other contexts. The literacy teacher's role is to focus on improving communication skills, but the teaching will inevitably take some people into new territories. It is hard to make people better communicators in a purely instrumental way; as people get better at it, they tend to find they have more to think about and more they want to say!

> I feel better about talking to my child's teacher now because I can speak the same language.

From *'Keeping up with the Kids'*,
Basic Skills May 1999, BSA

> In the workplace literacy and communication skills had to be demonstrated in 'real time'. There was usually no dummy run. Communication in different modes often took place virtually simultaneously and always had a real audience. Whatever the job and level of skills demanded, the ability to produce what was required in terms of communication was part of doing the job properly.

QCA, 1999, *Talking, Reading and Writing at Work*

ENTRY LEVEL 1

At this level, adults can

listen and respond
to spoken language, including simple narratives, statements, questions and single-step instructions

speak to communicate
basic information, feelings and opinions on familiar topics

engage in discussion
with another person in a familiar situation about familiar topics

in simple and familiar formal exchanges connected with education, training, work and social roles

---

Listen and respond	**SLlr/E1**

Skills, knowledge and understanding

Adults should be taught to:

❶ listen for the gist of short explanations

– understand the difference between listening for gist and listening for specific details and know which one is applicable in a situation

– use context clues and own experience to help understanding

– understand how to register engagement or interest in a face-to-face exchange, e.g. by body language, eye contact, facial expression

❷ listen for detail using key words to extract some specific information

– understand the importance of identifying the listening purpose and why the detail is needed

– understand that detail is obtained through listening for key words, e.g. names, places, times, dates, cost

– understand the importance of repeated words and phrases

– understand the difference between listening for detail face to face, where clarification can be sought, and listening to an impersonal announcement

❸ follow single-step instructions in a familiar context, asking for instructions to be repeated if necessary

– recognise and understand some key words used in instructions

– understand the need to be clear about what to do and how to ask for instructions to be repeated if necessary

❹ listen and respond to requests for personal information

– know and understand a range of contexts where people might legitimately be asked for personal information

– know likely key words associated with listening for and providing personal information

– know how to spell out their personal details for the listener if needed

Example

Follow the general sense of a short explanation, showing some sign of engagement, e.g. a briefing about a new course, a description of a holiday play scheme.

Listen and locate specific detail, e.g. the dates, times and location of classes when enrolling for a course, next month's targets for production or sales on a work shift.

Follow a simple spoken instruction correctly for work, leisure or study, e.g. for putting on basic safety clothing, for locking up after an event at a social centre.

Listen and respond to a request for personal details, e.g. request for name and address from a doctor's receptionist.

Sample activities

- With teacher or another learner identify some situations in their own life where listening for the gist of explanations is important, e.g.: the reasons for some sort of change at work; the purpose of an activity in a training session; accounts of plans, events, experiences by family members or friends.

- Practise listening and responding appropriately to short face-to-face explanations, e.g. listen to their teacher explain the importance of non-verbal communication and apply the principles to their own behaviour when listening.

- Use simple case studies, with their teacher taking on the role of information giver and learners listening for specific details that will provide information on *where, when, who, what* and *how*. For example: in a hospital outpatients, people are waiting for X-rays, ECGs, to see a particular consultant, book a new appointment, etc.; learners listen for their own announcement and act on it. As a group, they identify and discuss key words and what to do if relevant details are missed.

- Practise listening for single items of information in simulated, taped, short announcements, e.g.: travel details concerning bus/flight numbers, train platforms/destinations; prices and quantities from a market trader; patients' names and room numbers in a doctor's/dentist's waiting room.

- In pairs or in a group, identify the sort of key words to listen out for in instructions, e.g.: *put, place, push, pull, press, go to; on, over, under, next to, by, up, down.* Practise listening to single-step instructions, e.g. how to: use equipment, turn on a PC, type their user name and password to log on to the network, use the photocopier to copy a single sheet. Learners demonstrate their understanding by carrying out the tasks.

- In a group, learners listen to instructions from the teacher or on tape (e.g. concerning the safe use of cleaning equipment, when unused medicines should be taken or where they should be disposed of). The teacher checks understanding by asking *where, when, how, why, what* questions about the instructions and shows the group how to check their own understanding in this way, to identify any point they need to ask to be repeated.

- Use the speakerphone to get into a building, following the instruction, e.g. *Push the door when you hear the buzzer* or *Turn the handle now.*

- Discuss the different sorts of personal information people might be asked for and identify some questions. In pairs, practise listening to and giving information in familiar situations: one person asks or plays the tape of some simple questions (e.g. as a doctor's receptionist/patient; as a head teacher; a child's parent; as a post-office counter assistant/a customer) to the other, who responds; then change round. Compare and discuss.

- In pairs or groups, practise listening and responding to personal introductions in straightforward situations provided by the teacher, e.g.: as learners being introduced to a new class; as a parent being introduced to their son's/daughter's new girlfriend/boyfriend.

At this level, adults can

listen and respond
to spoken language, including simple narratives, statements, questions and single-step instructions

speak to communicate
basic information, feelings and opinions on familiar topics

engage in discussion
with another person in a familiar situation about familiar topics

in simple and familiar formal exchanges connected with education, training, work and social roles

Speak to communicate   SLc/E1

Skills, knowledge and understanding

Adults should be taught to:

1 speak clearly to be heard and understood in simple exchanges

- understand that effective communication depends on both speaker and listener, and the speaker must be aware of the needs of the listener
- be able to organise what is said so that the listener can follow, and speak loudly and clearly enough to be heard

2 make requests using appropriate terms

- understand that the manner in which requests are made can vary depending on how well the speaker knows the listener
- know and use some politeness conventions for making successful requests

3 ask questions to obtain specific information

- understand that the question needs to fit the purpose
- know how to frame simple questions in order to get the information required

4 make statements of fact clearly

- understand the importance of speaking clearly for the listener
- understand that context may affect how a statement of fact is said, e.g. the tone of voice for emphasis

Example

Explain a straightforward purpose clearly and appropriately in the context of work, leisure or study, e.g. to the teacher, explaining general aims for a job at the end of the course, to an elderly relative explaining how to re-heat a cooked meal.

Ask for help with a task in an appropriate manner, e.g. to put a suitcase on a rack, lift a buggy off a bus, find a place, complete a form.

Ask for specific information, e.g. about the cost of two or three types of the same product in a shop, about bus or train times from a station booking office.

Give factual information about themselves to another in a clear manner, e.g. when enrolling on a course, arriving for a dental appointment.

Engage in discussion   SLd/E1

In this section, it is expected that elements from both **Listen and respond** and **Speak to communicate** will be used as well as those shown below

Skills, knowledge and understanding

Adults should be taught to:

1 speak and listen in simple exchanges and everyday contexts

- understand that communication is a two-way, interactive process
- understand that non-verbal signals as well as spoken language contribute to communication between people

Example

Talk to a colleague about a task (in employment or voluntary work).

Greet familiar visitors, e.g. to the workplace, community centre, play group, learning centre.

Sample activities

- In pairs or groups, identify situations in everyday life where learners have found it hard to hear, distinguish or follow what someone else is saying. Discuss the reasons and together draw up some principles for effective one-to-one spoken communication, e.g.: hold head up and look at the listener; try to anticipate the listener's needs and think about what to say before plunging in; don't speak too quickly; use a polite tone to encourage a positive response, etc.

- Try putting agreed principles into practice. In pairs, conduct some simple exchanges provided by the teacher, e.g.: order a takeaway meal over the counter; describe some symptoms to the doctor; explain a problem a child is having at school to the teacher. Follow the same routine with each, i.e. consider the context, the position of the listener, the object of the exchange for the speaker.

- Record an answer-phone message on centre/work/home telephone or on a mobile phone.

- Ask learners in a group to identify from their own experience what they consider to be appropriate ways of having requests made to them in work, official, and social situations; from the feedback agree some *do*s and *don't*s for making requests.

- In pairs, applying *do*s and *don't*s, experiment with making the same request in different ways, distinguishing requests from commands and using appropriate politeness terms, e.g. asking a fellow learner to open the window/lend a pen; asking a stranger where the railway station is; asking the teacher to explain a point again; asking a manager if a shift can be changed.

- In a group, identify situations where learners need to ask questions for information, e.g. in shops, to ask for directions, at work, at the job centre. Outline a routine for obtaining information in such contexts: (a) identify precisely what information is needed; (b) turn that into a question or questions; (c) frame the question in a manner appropriate to the context. Practise the routine by asking sample questions to a partner in a variety of contexts.

- Encourage learners to ask questions in the learning situation, to obtain information and to clarify understanding, e.g. what to bring to the next session, when the holidays are, where to find resources.

- In pairs, learners make and tape statements about themselves, e.g. where they live, where they were born, their family, current or previous work/education/training, etc. Recordings can be used for individual review with a teacher on the confidence and clarity of their delivery.

- In pairs, experiment with making some statements of fact in different contexts, e.g.: tell a health-clinic receptionist details of a child's age, birth weight, etc.; tell a friend that their team has just lost and yours has won; tell a relative you can't baby sit because you have an evening class; tell a work colleague that they forgot to put some valuable equipment away.

Sample activities

- Identify greetings and partings used with family and friends. Consider which of these are also appropriate in other situations and what other forms are needed in other contexts, e.g. to greet a manager at work, a sales assistant, a receptionist, their child's teacher, a police officer, etc.

- Watch short video extracts of conversations in different contexts and observe non-verbal communication, e.g. body language, facial expressions, gestures, eye-contact. Discuss what they convey, e.g. lack of interest, attentiveness, amusement.

*At this level,
adults can*

listen and respond
to spoken language, including straightforward information, short narratives, explanations and instructions

speak to communicate
information, feelings and opinions on familiar topics

engage in discussion
with one or more people in a familiar situation to establish shared understanding about familiar topics

in straightforward familiar formal exchanges connected with education, training, work and social roles

Listen and respond	SLlr/E2

Skills, knowledge and understanding

Adults should be taught to:

❶ listen for and follow the gist of explanations, instructions and narratives

– recognise characteristic sequence markers and link words and use these to help follow order, e.g. *first of all, firstly, at the beginning, secondly, then, next, after a while, mean-while, finally, last of all, in the end*, etc.

❷ listen for detail in short explanations, instructions and narratives

– understand that key words and phrases vary with context

– recognise and understand the importance of key words used in familiar contexts, e.g. related to employment, travel, education and training

– understand and recognise some of the language characteristics of narratives, e.g. to describe people, places, events

❸ listen for and identify the main points of short explanations or presentations

– understand that identifying the main points means making a judgement about which parts are more important than the rest

– understand that it may be possible to identify the main points without remembering or understanding all the detail

– understand that speakers often provide clues to the main points, e.g. by tone of voice or repetition

❹ listen to and follow short, straightforward explanations and instructions

– understand that steps in instructions are to be followed in order

– understand sequential markers in instructions (e.g. *first, next, then*) and in explanations (e.g. *because, the reason for, so that*)

❺ listen to and identify simply expressed feelings and opinions

– recognise familiar language used to express positive and negative feelings and opinions, e.g. *I feel…, I like/don't like…, I think that…, I believe that…*

– understand that non-verbal communication can help to indicate a speaker's feelings and opinions (e.g. gesture, facial expression, sigh)

Example

Follow and understand an explanation, e.g. an account of new safety procedures at work.

Follow and take mental note of specific details in a local radio weather forecast or traffic update.

Listen to a short presentation on a project at work, in education or training, and relay the main points to a colleague.

Follow instructions from a health visitor for measuring a child's temperature and understand what action to take if necessary.

Listen and respond appropriately, e.g. to a fellow learner's feelings about a test or assignment, to a supervisor's comments about a job completed well.

Sample activities

- In pairs or groups, learners listen to a tape of people recounting their own experiences. They identify the general gist of each, discuss which are most effective in terms of clarity of speech and how easy to follow, then listen to these again, identifying together some features of effective spoken narratives.

- Listen to some interrupted taped extracts of familiar exchanges (e.g. doctor/patient, teacher/parent, parent/child, supervisor/worker, two friends). Identify the context and predict what might follow; give reasons for their predictions. Listen to the rest of the exchange to check; from the exercise formulate how listeners can pick up clues to general meaning.

- Use a computer to listen to the weather forecast on the local radio station to find out what the local weather will be like for the following day.

- Listen for detail in some taped descriptions of people, places, events, weather. Select from a pool of illustrations those that match the details in the descriptions heard.

- Identify situations where listening for detail is important. In pairs, practise listening for detail: one person listens to a short tape of relevant instructions or explanation (e.g. how to book a saver ticket in advance of a journey, changes to times for a class/event); they relay these to their partner as accurately as possible; both listen to the tape to check, then change roles for the next one.

- Listen to descriptions of some jobs (e.g. on tape, by the teacher, by other learners). Discuss in pairs or in a group and decide what the main duties of the jobs are.

- Discuss how speakers might emphasise their main points for listeners; listen to a short presentation (by a visitor, the teacher, or on tape, e.g. on an interesting visit, a community project). Listen for intonation, emphasis, repetition; identify the main points and compare judgements.

- Visit a news web site with a speech facility (e.g. Annanova.com) and find out the three main news stories.

- Follow simple staged instructions accompanied by a demonstration to complete different practical tasks, e.g. enlarging an image on a photocopier, copying a document to a floppy disk on a PC.

- In pairs, one person watches a short video clip of a TV cook or gardener giving an explanation of a process/action (e.g. why it is better to take eggs out of the fridge some time before using them, why you need to prepare the ground before planting potatoes). Watcher repeats the explanation to the other person as accurately as possible; both watch together to check.

- Give learners clear instructions related to their learning tasks. Ask them to check their understanding in pairs by comparing what each has understood, and to identify any points of uncertainty to be clarified with the teacher.

- Watch some short video clips from different TV programmes (documentaries, drama, soaps) where a person expresses feelings or opinions in an accessible way. Discuss what feelings or opinions are conveyed, and how (e.g. by language, intonation, gesture, facial expression).

- In pairs, role play some simple situations, identified as safe by the group, where one person expresses their opinion on a subject important to them (e.g. changes to some opening hours, to a payment system, to the school day). The other listens and summarises what they think the speaker feels and believes. The speaker judges how well the listener has understood.

listen and respond
to spoken language, including straightforward information, short narratives, explanations and instructions

speak to communicate
information, feelings and opinions on familiar topics

engage in discussion
with one or more people in a familiar situation to establish shared understanding about familiar topics

in straightforward familiar formal exchanges connected with education, training, work and social roles

Listen and respond — SLlr/E2

Skills, knowledge and understanding

Adults should be taught to:

6 respond to straightforward questions

– understand that an adequate response will depend on the type of question (e.g. simple *yes/no*, specific information)

– understand ways of making appropriate positive and negative responses to questions

– give clear responses that the listener can follow

Example

Respond appropriately to questions about familiar things, e.g. from an assessor observing a learning task, from a supervisor about what went well or badly on a task.

Speak to communicate — SLc/E2

Skills, knowledge and understanding

Adults should be taught to:

1 speak clearly to be heard and understood in straightforward exchanges

– understand that the speaker should take account of the needs of the listener, by speaking to others clearly, audibly and intelligibly

– know and follow some principles for clear effective one-to-one exchanges

Example

Speak clearly in an effective short exchange (e.g. to a colleague back from their holiday, explaining which jobs have been completed while they were away; to a counter assistant, giving the reasons for wanting to change some goods).

2 make requests and ask questions to obtain information in everyday contexts

– understand that questions need to be framed so as to suit the context and the nature of the information sought

– know and use various politeness forms appropriate to the context to obtain information from others

Obtain some straightforward information, e.g. from their line manager on how to book holiday dates, from a travel adviser about a particular holiday.

3 express clearly statements of fact, and short accounts and descriptions

– understand that meaning must be expressed clearly for the listener to follow, and act on if necessary

– understand that the amount of information and the style of account or description will depend on the context

Describe symptoms clearly to a doctor.

Give an account of problems with a car to the person who is going to mend it.

4 ask questions to clarify understanding

– know and use some strategies to clarify and confirm understanding, e.g. ask for information to be repeated, ask follow-on questions

Recognise when clarification is needed and ask appropriate follow-on questions, e.g. when placing an order in a store, opening a building society account, when asking directions to a ward on visiting someone in hospital.

Sample activities

- Investigate how to recognise when questions are being asked, and the type of response they invite. In pairs or in a group, listen to a tape of questions with different structures and intonations, e.g. *where, when, why, who, what* questions; *have you, did you, are you, will you; so you will/won't/might/can't*. Identify some patterns and see which invite open and which closed responses, and recognise the sorts of questions that are more likely to occur in certain situations.

- Identify some familiar situations where questions are asked. In pairs, role play a situation (e.g. answer questions from: a plumber/electrician/DIY expert on the location and nature of a fault; a family member about a holiday/social event; a workmate about what happened in their absence). Reverse roles and review their own and each other's answers.

Sample activities

- Identify in a group some situations from daily life where it is important to speak clearly, audibly and intelligibly (e.g. when making a request or complaint, confirming arrangements, agreeing a procedure at work, explaining something to someone who needs to know). Recap on principles for clear, effective communication. In pairs, conduct a given exchange (e.g. ask the bin men why they have missed emptying the rubbish for the last two weeks; explain a child's absence to a teacher). One person leads with the other as listener/responder; reverse roles with another situation and review their own and each other's talk for clarity, appropriateness and the response of the listener.

- Discuss how the group operates when engaged in group discussion and when talking with the teacher. Identify any areas for development.

- Choose a context of relevance to learners and, in pairs or in a small group, prepare a short list of questions to obtain required information (e.g. about adult education courses and fees from an advice centre, about a child's progress from a teacher, about reasons for symptoms from a doctor, about flats to rent in a given price range from a letting agent). In pairs, try out the questions on each other in role.

- Watch some video clips and identify situations where information is sought in work, home or social contexts. Then in pairs, using prompt cards, practise asking for information in everyday contexts, each taking turns to be the questioner.

- In pairs, look at some illustrations of familiar objects (e.g. a telescope, CD player, mobile phone, barbecue set, fishing rod). Describe them to each other clearly, saying what they are for and (in simple terms) how they work. The listener gives feedback on the clarity of the statements, the use of 'fillers', repetition, hesitation, etc.

- In pairs, learners give short narrative recounts of their own daily/weekly routine. They compare and discuss both accounts; identify what makes a good account and pool suggestions in the whole group.

- In pairs or in a group, listen to some short taped exchanges where the questioner has to clarify or needs more information; identify some follow-up questions and frame them appropriately, e.g.:

  Q.   *Could you tell me where the Odeon Cinema is, please?*

  A.   *Yes, just go down West Street, and it's on your right.*

  Q.   (thinks) *Where's West Street.....?*

  Follow up question: *Thanks – could you point me towards West Street, please?*

- Listen to an explanation from the teacher (e.g. on word processing their own work) and discuss some ways of seeking clarification, e.g. repeating a section as a question: *So you must save your work every five minutes?*, *Can I just check that you said we have to save our work every five minutes?*, asking *what if* questions: *What happens if you press delete by mistake?*

At this level, adults can

listen and respond
to spoken language, including straightforward information, short narratives, explanations and instructions

speak to communicate
information, feelings and opinions on familiar topics

engage in discussion
with one or more people in a familiar situation to establish shared understanding about familiar topics

in straightforward familiar formal exchanges connected with education, training, work and social roles

Engage in discussion   SLd/E2

In this section, it is expected that elements from both **Listen and respond** and **Speak to communicate** will be used as well as those shown below

Skills, knowledge and understanding	**Example**
Adults should be taught to:	
❶ follow the gist of discussions – be able to understand the general sense of a discussion by listening to what others say	Follow a discussion in class between the teacher and the group, understand the conclusions reached, and act on them if necessary.
❷ follow the main points and make appropriate contributions to the discussion – listen and be able to distinguish the main points from the detail – understand that appropriate contributions relate to the topic of conversation	Follow the main points in a class discussion and make a relevant contribution.

Sample activities

- Listen to a short taped extract of a simple discussion (can be of their own class on a previous occasion). In pairs, summarise to each other the subject of the discussion and identify any conclusions/outcomes/follow-up actions. Pool findings with the rest of the group and consider any differences between following a discussion and a one-to-one exchange (e.g. it may not always be clear in a discussion how one contribution links to another).

- Watch a short video clip of a discussion (e.g. from a talk show). As a group, compare watching discussion on video with listening to a tape. Identify what factors might help the listener follow the discussion (e.g. body language, facial expressions) and what might hinder them (e.g. being distracted by people's appearance, dress or mannerisms).

- Practise following the main points and building confidence to make contributions by listening to two or three minutes of an audio tape of a straightforward discussion on a topic of current interest (e.g. from the radio or of another class). At the end of the tape continue the discussion in pairs for two minutes. Join with another pair, ask them their views and continue the discussion in a foursome for two more minutes.

- Hold a 'hot spot' session every other week (e.g. in the coffee break) where a learner or teacher comes with a current 'hot' topic from local or national news, introduces the topic and asks the group for their views. Hold an informal 5–10 minute discussion where the rule is that everyone must make at least one contribution. The teacher sums up (or asks a learner, if appropriate) and seeks a volunteer to provide next time's hot topic.

*At this level,
adults can*

listen and respond
to spoken language, including
straightforward information and
narratives, and follow
straightforward explanations and
instructions, both face to face and
on the telephone

speak to communicate
information, feelings and opinions
on familiar topics, using
appropriate formality, both face to
face and on the telephone

engage in discussion
with one or more people in a
familiar situation, making relevant
points and responding to what
others say to reach a shared
understanding about familiar
topics

in familiar formal exchanges
connected with education,
training, work and social roles

Listen and respond

SLlr/E3

Skills, knowledge and understanding

Adults should be taught to:

**❶ listen for and follow the gist of
explanations, instructions and
narratives in different contexts**

- know how to listen for gist, making use of
  their own knowledge, context clues, linking
  words and sequence markers
- understand that listening on the phone can
  be more demanding than face-to-face
  listening (usually less knowledge of the
  context, no visual clues, so more reliance
  on hearing)

**❷ listen for detail in explanations,
instructions and narratives in different
contexts**

- use key words to clue into a particular topic
- focus listening in relation to purpose
- understand the differences between
  listening for detail in real time on the
  telephone, and listening to recorded
  messages which can be replayed

**❸ listen for and identify relevant
information and new information from
discussions, explanations and
presentations**

- understand that judging the relevance of
  information will depend on the context and
  purpose of the listening
- understand the need to register new
  information in order to decide whether it is
  relevant or not
- understand that significant points are often
  emphasised, repeated, or summarised at
  the end of an explanation or presentation

**❹ use strategies to clarify and confirm
understanding (e.g. facial expressions
or gestures)**

- understand that a listener can signal
  response to a speaker using visual and
  verbal signals depending on context
- know and use some feedback signals to
  check understanding when listening
  face to face

Example

Listen for gist in different contexts, e.g. in a
large group at a talk to parents about a school
trip, at a union meeting, or on the telephone
to follow up why an expected delivery did not
arrive.

Listen to a message on a telephone
answering machine and pass on details to
another person.

Listen at work (face to face or on the
telephone) to a complaint from a customer, to
decide who should deal with it.

Follow a demonstration of some equipment
(e.g. in a store or at work), signalling
understanding and querying by confirming
statements, questions and non-verbal signs.

Sample activities

- Listen for the gist of an explanation or narrative on a short video clip (e.g. from a TV popular science, technology or consumer affairs programme). In pairs, learners briefly summarise what they have picked up under appropriate headings (e.g. general topic area, who or what is involved, any outcomes, any questions for future). Pool points for discussion, with the teacher summarising overall gist. (They can watch again to identify specific detail.)

- In pairs or in a group, listen for gist to an audio tape from various contexts (e.g. an automated answering service, a call to a telephone helpline, a customer enquiring about information on travel or a product/service). Each learner identifies the context and topic and cross-checks with their partner.

- In a group, identify situations in daily life where listening for detail takes place; then listen to clips from local radio (weather forecast, travel information, venues for events, adverts, special offers, sales, etc.). Ask learners to remember as much detail as they can, then discuss what different people have remembered. Identify why it is easier to listen for detail in a particular context and when there is a 'need to know' (e.g. details of local travel when out on the road, local weather forecasts when deciding whether to have a barbecue supper, instructions when they need to carry them out).

- In pairs, one person listens for detail to a short message on an answering machine (e.g. time and place to meet, a contact name or number) and tries to describe orally to partner; both listen to check accuracy. Identify when it is necessary to make a note of specific details to be able to remember them; reverse roles and listen to a different type of message and style of caller. Pool responses for a discussion on listening for and noting details.

- Discuss how to decide whether information is relevant. Learners reflect on recent listening situations and identify listening purpose (or lack of). Using a video clip or a short live presentation, learners listen for a specific purpose, identify and if necessary note down key points relevant to them (e.g. from a presentation by the head of centre about courses for the coming year/term).

- In a group, and in the context of researching a common topic to prepare some writing (e.g. letters to a local newspaper on a contentious issue), listeners follow a video/audio clip and listen for information that is new and relevant to the task. Discuss the information and its relevance, then listen again, making notes of useful points, e.g. dates, figures.

- Discuss in a group how a listener might convey various reactions (such as puzzlement, agreement, checking understanding) to a speaker face to face, e.g. by facial expressions, gestures such as pointing, nodding, comments such as *I see, yes, ah, Does that mean that...?, What about...? What if...* , etc. Discuss differences when checking and confirming understanding on the telephone. Rehearse some strategies in pairs.

- Follow an explanation/demonstration by teacher (e.g. changing a printer cartridge, finding a particular web site/section of a reference book), confirming and checking understanding by facial expression, gesture, confirming remarks, checking questions to feed back to the speaker. Afterwards check out if teacher's impression matched learners' reactions and, if not, why not.

At this level, adults can

listen and respond
to spoken language, including straightforward information and narratives, and follow straightforward explanations and instructions, both face to face and on the telephone

speak to communicate
information, feelings and opinions on familiar topics, using appropriate formality, both face to face and on the telephone

engage in discussion
with one or more people in a familiar situation, making relevant points and responding to what others say to reach a shared understanding about familiar topics

in familiar formal exchanges connected with education, training, work and social roles

---

Listen and respond · SLlr/E3

Skills, knowledge and understanding

Adults should be taught to:

⑤ listen to and respond appropriately to other points of view

– understand the tendency for people to listen less carefully to points of view different from their own

– know some strategies for paying attention to other points of view and for responding appropriately even when disagreeing with the viewpoint

Example

Listen to opposing viewpoints in a meeting and make their own contribution using the appropriate meeting conventions (e.g. tenants' association meeting).

⑥ respond to a range of questions about familiar topics

– understand that questions can come in different forms, which affect the kind of response required

– understand that the sorts of question will vary depending on the context and situation

Respond to questions about their own experiences, e.g. a teacher's questions about a group visit, a union representative's questions about how new health and safety procedures are going.

Speak to communicate · SLc/E3

Skills, knowledge and understanding

Adults should be taught to:

❶ speak clearly to be heard and understood using appropriate clarity, speed and phrasing

– understand that pace of delivery affects clarity of speech and how easily the listener can hear and follow (e.g. speaking too quickly, or with too much hesitation)

– understand that appropriate speed and phrasing will depend to some extent on context

– be able to speak clearly and appropriately over short periods

Example

Make a contribution to an informal meeting which is clear, audible and appropriately paced, e.g. giving vote of thanks to fire officers for visiting neighbourhood fundraising event.

❷ use formal language and register when appropriate

– understand that spoken language has different registers, depending on the formality of the situation and on the relationship between the speakers

– be able to shift registers for different familiar contexts and situations

Formally welcome an outside visitor at a meeting or event.

Sample activities

- Watch some short video clips of people expressing their points of view in different contexts (e.g. in House of Commons, TV discussion show, a work meeting on a training video, discussion from a soap). Discuss how the people involved conveyed their responses to other viewpoints and decide how well they were listening. In a group, identify a list of *do*s and *don't*s; each person then considers which of these applies to them in their own listening.

- As a follow-on group activity, identify some strategies to prevent 'listening shut down', e.g.: by not interrupting/exclaiming; by imagining having to recount the point of view accurately to another person; by trying to compare it with their own view. Pool some useful phrases for responding appropriately to other points of view, e.g.: *that's a fair point, I'd not thought of it that way; that's very interesting but ...; I see what you mean but ...; that's one way of looking at things ...; I agree with your point that, but ...; I'm not sure I understand why you think that ... I disagree with everything/most of/some of what's been said because ...*

- Explore some of the conventions of questions and responses in different situations by listening to a tape or to the teacher reading out examples (e.g. from a job interview, a marriage ceremony, a consumer survey, a manager seeking feedback on a new procedure, a colleague asking for another's opinion). Identify different ways of framing questions and discuss how to respond (e.g. *Can you tell me a bit about your experience of . . . ?* is an invitation to talk; *What do you think about Jack's point?* probably needs more than a one-word answer).

- In pairs, practise responding to questions that require different degrees of response, using prepared question cards related to familiar contexts, e.g. *What do you think about those plans to build a new sports centre next to the school? Which of these statements best describes your food shopping habits? Are you going to enrol for this class again next year?* etc.

- Ring Directory Enquiries and ask for the number of e.g. the learning centre, the station, a friend.

Sample activities

- In pairs, listen to a tape made from radio phone-ins and discuss the contributions for their clarity, audibility, pace, choice of expressions; pool findings for a discussion on features of effective and less effective contributions.

- In pairs, identify and share experiences of some situations where speaking clearly with the right volume and pace is particularly important (e.g. reporting back at a meeting, making announcement/giving vote of thanks at an event, answering questions in an interview). Each person chooses a situation they would like to practise (e.g. explaining reasons for applying for a job if they have an interview pending). Talk over what needs to be said, then practise with partner and when ready tape each other's contribution. Listen to and review with teacher.

- Use a tape recorder or computer voice-recognition program to read and record a story to be included as tape, floppy disk or CD in a Storysack.

- Discuss as a group how language varies between informal and more formal settings, e.g. differences in conversations with a colleague who is also a friend, when at work and when in a social setting. In pairs, identify situations in their own lives where more formal language is needed. Pool examples and discuss as a group the sort of language that could be used in those situations.

- Listen to an audio tape of people speaking. In pairs, try to identify the context and situation from the sort of language they are using (e.g. from a public speech, a meeting, an informal discussion, an interview); report back answers and discuss. With partner rehearse a formal exchange and a less formal one (e.g. introduce the topic and purpose of a formal meeting; introduce a new colleague to a team of workers/volunteers).

- Telephone and leave an answer-phone message for a friend at home; then leave a message on the shared work answer-phone.

At this level,
adults can

listen and respond
to spoken language, including
straightforward information and
narratives, and follow
straightforward explanations and
instructions, both face to face and
on the telephone

speak to communicate
information, feelings and opinions
on familiar topics, using
appropriate formality, both face to
face and on the telephone

engage in discussion
with one or more people in a
familiar situation, making relevant
points and responding to what
others say to reach a shared
understanding about familiar
topics

in familiar formal exchanges
connected with education,
training, work and social roles

Speak to communicate	SLc/E3

Skills, knowledge and understanding

Adults should be taught to:

3 express clearly statements of fact
and give short explanations, accounts
and descriptions

– use knowledge of context and situation to
judge the level of detail required

– understand that sticking to the point is
usually a factor in successful short
explanations, accounts and descriptions

– understand that, as well as facts, opinions
and feelings may form part of explanations,
accounts, descriptions, depending on
context and situation

4 make requests and ask questions to
obtain information in familiar and
unfamiliar contexts

– know how to make requests and ask
questions clearly and simply so the listener
understands what information is required

– know some strategies for clarifying and
confirming understanding, especially when
speaking over the telephone

– know and use suitable politeness
conventions, and formal language and
register where appropriate

Example

Give an explanation clearly and at the right
level of detail, e.g. to a new colleague on how
and where to find information about team
meetings, to new learners on how to arrange
appointments with the teacher.

Make a telephone enquiry and obtain
information required, e.g. about time of a film,
availability and cost of tickets for an event,
cost of a service.

Engage in discussion	SLd/E3

In this section, it is expected that elements from both **Listen and respond** and **Speak to communicate** will
be used as well as those shown below

Skills, knowledge and understanding

Adults should be taught to:

1 follow and understand the main
points of discussions on different
topics

– understand that discussion can serve
different purposes, e.g. to share views,
plan a task, solve a problem, clear the air

– understand that discussion does not always
follow a linear sequence

– be able to listen with some concentration
to grasp main points

Example

Follow a news interview on local radio and be
able to form a view on the issue.

Sample activities

- Discuss how the amount of information and level of detail might depend on situation. Pool relevant situations from their own experience, e.g. giving information to emergency services on the telephone, correct details when booking holiday, explanation of work routines to new colleague, account of accident to A&E department, description of damage to loss adjuster. In pairs, using some given situations, practise appropriate responses, including giving opinion or feelings if relevant.

- Practise recounting, explaining and describing incidents, processes, places clearly and succinctly (using video clips as stimulus as necessary). Think about where to begin and end and what to include, then speak within a strict time limit. The listener judges if the speaker has conveyed the critical information in the time.

- As a group, identify situations where they use the telephone to obtain information, and share any difficulties encountered (e.g. speaking, listening and writing at the same time, hanging up having forgotten to ask a crucial question). In pairs, simulate asking for information on the telephone, including checking and clarifying (e.g. travel times and fares, choice of dates of events and price of tickets, availability and cost of goods and services). Review information obtained and judge how successful the enquiry was.

- Discuss what is involved in finding out information in unfamiliar contexts (e.g. not sure what questions to ask, not wanting to appear foolish). As a group identify what they would like information about (e.g. a newly opened fitness centre), generate some useful questions (e.g. re facilities, charges, hours) and decide how best to get answers (e.g. phone and ask for a brochure; ask to look round and go along with another person to help listen to answers). In pairs, plan some routines for seeking information in other unfamiliar but useful contexts.

- Prepare and record in advance some questions for a parents' evening, including questions on a child's general progress, their friends (and other social issues), and the next year's teacher.

- Telephone the Train Information Service for times of trains to the nearest large city.

Sample activities

- Identify situations where a discussion might take place and for what purposes. Watch some short video clips to follow the main points and consider the purpose (e.g. sports programme discussion on football hooliganism, workplace discussion from a training video). Pool findings and consider how well the discussions served their purpose.

- In a group, learners are briefed to listen for and identify main opposing views in a video-taped discussion in which people express strong opinions, and also to note the way people express themselves (including body language). Share findings and discuss how easy it was to follow the discussion. Think of further points that could be made in support of or against those on tape.

ENTRY 3 LEVEL *At this level, adults can*

listen and respond
to spoken language, including straightforward information and narratives, and follow straightforward explanations and instructions, both face to face and on the telephone

speak to communicate
information, feelings and opinions on familiar topics, using appropriate formality, both face to face and on the telephone

engage in discussion
with one or more people in a familiar situation, making relevant points and responding to what others say to reach a shared understanding about familiar topics

in familiar formal exchanges connected with education, training, work and social roles

Engage in discussion   SLd/E3

Skills, knowledge and understanding

Adults should be taught to:

❷ make contributions to discussions that are relevant to the subject

– make contributions at the appropriate time, i.e. following on from the previous point, not several points back

– know and use phrases that help relate their own contribution to others' in discussions with more than one person

❸ respect the turn-taking rights of others during discussions

– understand that productive discussion involves people speaking one at a time

– understand that people can use eye contact and gestures to help signal that they would like to speak next

Example

Make useful contributions to a planning meeting for a community event, e.g. a fundraising activity, celebration.

Take part in a discussion, making some relevant contributions but not talking over others, e.g. planning a group research project with fellow learners, evaluating the success of a family literacy course with other participants.

Sample activities

- Plan a discussion for the following week so that learners have time to think about the points they wish to raise, preferably on a real issue (e.g. to get views on centre opening times/childcare facilities/access to computers). Teacher chairs the discussion and gives individuals feedback about their contributions.

- After watching a taped discussion, identify the sorts of phrases people used to link their contributions to others' *(I'd like to support what Ken said, Picking up Diane's point, Following on from that,* etc).

- Identify some well known 'discussion hoggers' from TV and public life and discuss why they make it difficult for others to get a word in edgeways. Then watch a video discussion where some participants dominate and do not take turns to speak. Discuss their behaviour and its effect on the discussion.

- Recap on useful phrases to link their own to others' contribution, and on expressions and body language that signal a wish to speak, then take part in an unchaired discussion in which the rules are that everybody has to make at least two contributions and only one person speaks at once. Appoint one member of the group as an observer who reports at the end.

See also in the key skills: Communication key skills level 1
Part A: In discussions. . .
Part B: C1.1

At this level, adults can

listen and respond
to spoken language, including information and narratives, and follow explanations and instructions of varying lengths, adapting response to speaker, medium and context

speak to communicate
information, ideas and opinions adapting speech and content to take account of the listener(s) and medium

engage in discussion
with one or more people in familiar and unfamiliar situations, making clear and relevant contributions that respond to what others say and produce a shared understanding about different topics

in formal exchanges connected with education, training, work and social roles

Listen and respond

Skills, knowledge and understanding

Adults should be taught to:

1 listen for and identify relevant information from explanations and presentations on a range of straightforward topics
  – understand that relevance will depend on listening purpose, context or task

2 listen for and understand explanations, instructions and narratives on different topics in a range of contexts
  – understand the importance of sustaining concentration and listening to the end to get overall understanding
  – understand the different listening demands when listening face to face, in a large group, and on the telephone

3 use strategies to clarify and confirm understanding (e.g. facial expressions, body language and verbal prompts)
  – understand listener can use visual and verbal signals to confirm or query understanding with speaker
  – know and use some strategies to check their own understanding

4 provide feedback and confirmation when listening to others
  – understand that speakers need feedback from listeners to gauge the effect of what they are saying and make adjustments if necessary
  – know and use some visual and aural feedback signals when listening face to face and on the telephone

5 make contributions relevant to the situation and the subject
  – understand that it is necessary to listen carefully in order to make relevant contributions at the right time

SLlr/L1

Example

Listen to a presentation and identify information relevant to their own situation (e.g. for parents about how to apply for a child's secondary school place).

Listen to, understand and be able to perform a set of instructions, e.g. on how to give the kiss of life from a demonstration on a dummy.

Use appropriate clarifying non-verbal and verbal signals to make sure of understanding when listening one to one or in a small group to some instructions, e.g. new procedures for completing time sheets, for receiving benefit payments.

Listen with obvious engagement face to face while someone explains or recounts something (e.g. a job of work that has to be done, a situation that has to be tackled).

Contribute usefully to a conversation to plan something in a work, community or study context, e.g. a team discussion about providing back-up in a particular job, an activity-planning session with fellow learners.

Sample activities

- Practise locating and noting down specific information from recorded messages, using real systems or tapes of them (e.g. find out the times of a particular film from information on the week's screenings at local multiplex, select required option to obtain information about a particular holiday destination). Discuss advantages and disadvantages of these systems.

- In the context of collecting information for a group discussion on a topical issue, listen to recent radio and video clips and make brief notes on points to use, e.g. facts and figures in support of a view, names of organisations or groups involved, names of main people involved.

- Set up a telephone or on-line audio-conference call with two others (e.g. between learners at other centres, in a workplace scenario, to home) to discuss and, for example, decide where and when to meet, make arrangements for holding a Christmas party, resolve a work problem.

- Consider in a group whether listening for pleasure and entertainment is different from listening for business, work or learning; then listen to the opening of a story or novel read by the teacher or from a tape. Share responses on where the story is set, who is involved, what might happen next. If interest is aroused, listen to further episodes in following weeks.

- Practise listening to and following instructions or explanations by working in pairs. One person goes out of room; other watches a video clip (e.g. DIY, current affairs, travel programme) then explains it to partner. They watch again together to see how much was passed on, and how accurately. In a group, discuss some tips for improving listening concentration, e.g. listen for and try to remember three main points/something from the beginning, middle and end/associate points with visual clues or humour.

- Discuss how listeners can check that what they are hearing is the same as the speaker is trying to get across (nodding, signalling uncertainty, e.g. by screwing up forehead to look puzzled, *umming* and *arring*, *mmming*, *Does that mean that? Is that because…, What do I do if, Can you just say that again, please?*). Compare strategies for face-to-face and telephone contexts.

- In pairs, try out some situations; the speaker reports on whether they could tell if the listener was following what was said or not.

- Use a video-conferencing facility to conduct a discussion with students from other centres on a current news topic, or to discuss progress in learning/new ICT program. Review a tape of the discussion and compare the strategies used to confirm understanding.

- Compare how a listener might provide feedback and confirmation face to face and on the telephone (e.g. nodding, smiling, *I see, Yes, I understand, Go on,* etc.). Listen to some video and telephone clips and make a note of examples of different types of feedback. Discuss with partner.

- With two other learners, practise some situations (using case study cards or titles from teacher) where listener gives appropriate feedback to speaker face to face and on telephone (using training phones). Take turns to be the observer who reports back on feedback signals observed. Discuss and change round.

- Consider as a group what it means to 'talk at cross purposes' (the comedy film *Airplane* has some good examples) and share their own experiences. Identify some *do*s and *don't*s to avoid the situation (e.g. DO: listen properly, think about context and purpose of talk, use what other person says as a starting point for own contributions; DON'T: ignore what the other person is saying, 'talk at random', i.e. saying the first thing that comes into your head or something you want to say but which has nothing to do with the subject!).

- With two other learners, practise listening and responding with relevant contributions using some sample starting lines of conversation (from familiar work or social contexts, e.g. how to raise money for a community facility). Keep the conversation going, developing, confirming, adding relevant new point to previous speakers'. One person observes how well the others do it; then change roles.

LEVEL 1 *At this level, adults can*

listen and respond
to spoken language, including information and narratives, and follow explanations and instructions of varying lengths, adapting response to speaker, medium and context

speak to communicate
information, ideas and opinions adapting speech and content to take account of the listener(s) and medium

engage in discussion
with one or more people in familiar and unfamiliar situations, making clear and relevant contributions that respond to what others say and produce a shared understanding about different topics

in formal exchanges connected with education, training, work and social roles

Listen and respond

SLlr/L1

Skills, knowledge and understanding

Adults should be taught to:

6 **respond to questions on a range of topics**

– know that questions come in a variety of forms depending on context and topic

– understand the expectations that different sorts of questions convey, and respond appropriately

Example

Take part in an interview answering questions appropriately, to give a good account of their own experience and skills (e.g. for paid or voluntary work, or an education/training place).

Speak to communicate

SLc/L1

Skills, knowledge and understanding

Adults should be taught to:

1 **speak clearly in a way which suits the situation**

– understand that pace, volume and precision of articulation vary depending on the situation (speaking face to face, on the telephone, to a group)

Example

Speak clearly in a small team so as to be heard and understood, e.g. in a meeting to plan a street party.

2 **make requests and ask questions to obtain information in familiar and unfamiliar contexts**

– know how to make requests and ask questions to get required information, adapting level of formality to situation and context

Ask for information about rights and entitlements, e.g. from a union representative, the Citizen's Advice Bureau, a Housing Officer.

3 **express clearly statements of fact, explanations, instructions, accounts, and descriptions**

– know how to match content and level of detail to context and situation

– understand that, to convey meaning clearly in talk of more than a few moments, it is necessary to sustain concentration and keep the thread running

Give a set of clear instructions for completing a task (e.g. hanging wallpaper) to someone doing it for the first time, so they are able to follow and understand.

Sample activities

- Rehearse answering questions in the context of an interview. Watch a training video extract to identify unsatisfactory responses (e.g. information not in logical order; insufficient detail, so interviewer has to keep probing; too much detail, which loses listener's attention). Discuss observations and draw up a list of *do*s and *don't*s to use in interview simulations.

- Making use of knowledge in their own daily life or researched for reading/writing activities in class, hold a periodic 'ask the expert' slot. Members of the group volunteer to answer questions on a subject they have been investigating or are knowledgeable about (e.g. best buys in camcorders, how to use a fork-lift truck safely, what training is needed to be a first aider at work, a topic of local history). The 'expert' gives a brief introduction to set context then answers questions for five minutes. Follow with a short discussion on the question types (e.g. did they concentrate on facts, ask about feelings/opinions/experience or for advice?) and how the speaker responded.

Sample activities

- Listen to some audio clips of people speaking and, from the speed of delivery, emphasis, volume, decide on the context and situation (e.g. a politician speaking to a crowd, a speech of thanks, an extract from a play, from a discussion, from a 'chat'). Discuss situations in their own lives where different degrees of clarity are needed (e.g. making an announcement, speaking to the boss, addressing a parents' group, speaking to a young child or a very old person).

- In pairs, select some situation cards and discuss the best sort of delivery for the situation (e.g. speaking on a crackling mobile phone in a room full of people, asking for quiet for a speaker, delivering an important message so as not to disturb others, explaining a point to a manager, dissuading a child from doing something dangerous at playgroup).

- Prepare questions to ask of a visiting speaker on a pre-arranged topic, e.g. a union representative, a housing officer, a community police officer, an employer, a health worker, a careers advisor, etc.

- Agree some information to be obtained by telephone between lessons; learners then report back to the group on the process and on the information obtained (e.g. on childcare facilities, part-time vacancies at a local supermarket).

- Telephone Learndirect to ask about possible 'next steps' in learning. Give details of current course, interests, availability, etc.

- In pairs, consider a range of given situations and decide what content would be needed, how to organise it, how much detail and how the way of expressing content might need to be adapted to context (e.g. explaining a property repair problem to a landlord over the phone, rules of a game to a small child, account of an incident to the police). Rehearse some of the situations together.

- Use a short video or audio clip (1 to 2 minutes) of someone explaining or recounting a process or happening. Play once to get general sense of content, then play again, listening particularly for how the speaker has kept the thread running so the whole piece makes sense (e.g. linking words or phrases such as *then, after, as well as, another thing*). In pairs, practise speaking for at least a minute without losing the thread or repeating points (e.g. explain a current project to do with home, work or study).

The Adult Literacy
Core Curriculum

See also in the key skills:

Communication key skills level 1
Part A: In discussions...
Part B: C1.1

At this level, adults can

listen and respond
to spoken language, including information and narratives, and follow explanations and instructions of varying lengths, adapting response to speaker, medium and context

speak to communicate
information, ideas and opinions adapting speech and content to take account of the listener(s) and medium

engage in discussion
with one or more people in familiar and unfamiliar situations, making clear and relevant contributions that respond to what others say and produce a shared understanding about different topics

in formal exchanges connected with education, training, work and social roles

Speak to communicate | SLc/L1

Skills, knowledge and understanding

Adults should be taught to:

4 present information and ideas in a logical sequence and include detail and develop ideas where appropriate

– understand that speakers need to organise, sequence and link what they say so that listeners can follow

– understand that main points and ideas can be supported and developed with details (e.g. examples, evidence)

Example

Give an account of an appointment with a prospective employer to a Job Centre assistant, organising information coherently and including details where relevant (e.g. of start dates, wages, hours).

Engage in discussion | SLd/L1

In this section, it is expected that elements from both **Listen and respond** and **Speak to communicate** will be used as well as those shown below

Skills, knowledge and understanding

Adults should be taught to:

1 follow and contribute to discussions on a range of straightforward topics

– understand that a discussion can be affected by the nature of its purpose and that their own purpose may differ from that of others

– know how to respond appropriately to other points of view

Example

Participate in a local meeting, e.g. residents'/tenants' association, community organisation.

2 respect the turn-taking rights of others during discussions

– understand that an effective discussion involves everyone having a fair chance to make their contributions

– know and use some strategies to signal to others that they can speak (facial expression, gesture, phrases)

Take part in a discussion with other learners on a sensitive subject and get their own points across while not shouting others down (e.g. on whether it is right that families can be evicted if their children cause trouble in the neighbourhood).

3 use appropriate phrases for interruption

– know what to say to create an opportunity to make a contribution at an appropriate time

Make contributions at a public meeting, e.g. about a planning application for a night club, neighbourhood crime prevention.

Sample activities

- Practise organising information and ideas to present to other learners (e.g. on a topic related to work, training, study, hobby). Identify five or six main points and make a note of them; sequence the points in a logical order, with an introduction, some development and a conclusion, and think about how to move from one point to the next (e.g. by linking words: *firstly, secondly, finally, however, therefore, nevertheless*, etc.). Using notes as aide-mémoire if necessary, present the information to partner. Pool feedback and, as a group, identify features of well-structured talk.

- Take a contentious statement (e.g. *people should not be allowed to beg on the street).* In pairs, identify three points for and three against the statement; for each point think of some supporting details, such as examples or evidence from own observations/knowledge. One person organises the points for and the other the points against; pairs present supported points to the group in a logical order. Compare and discuss points raised.

- Prepare a presentation using voice-over (e.g. on Slideshow builder, Coursebuilder, Powerpoint or similar), for example for new parents to a primary school.

Sample activities

- Investigate what makes a discussion effective. Watch a video discussion and observe how participants respond to other points of view. Compare and contrast appropriate and inappropriate responses (in same or different videos) and identify some features of appropriate responses (e.g. try to link own contribution to others', try to follow on from the last point, only change direction if relevant, and say so).

- Divide learners into small groups (three or four) and provide a task that requires discussion and agreement with a time limit, e.g. plan an end-of-term celebration and agree what, when, how to fund it; allocate roles. Appoint one person as observer who reports on how well group managed the discussion (e.g. talking one at a time, focusing on the task, no long pauses, making useful and well-timed contributions, responding constructively to each other's suggestions, being willing to re-consider own view point, etc.).

- Watch a video discussion and count each person's significant speaking turns (ignore *yes, no, mmm*, etc.); each group member can be allocated a person 'to count'. Compare results (was anyone dominant? was there anyone who didn't contribute? anyone who tried but didn't manage to?). Discuss possible reasons for each person's different levels of participation (e.g. degree of confidence, interest, subject knowledge, not sufficiently assertive, other people too dominant, etc.).

- Following on from this, identify some 'turn-taking tips' for use in their own discussions (e.g. sit in a circle so it is easier for all to be aware of everyone and no one can hide; encourage less confident speakers; try using 'hard stares' on those who talk too much; keep tabs on own contributions – don't opt out but don't dominate; use your contribution to draw in someone else.

- Watch video discussions or interviews that provide good models for appropriate interruption and identify the features, e.g. choosing right time, picking up on what current speaker is saying to provide a lead-in for own contribution or others'.

- Using turn-taking tips and phrases for interrupting, members consider how they can use them to develop own discussions skills (e.g. being more aware of others, not 'switching off', not getting too 'carried away', retaining concentration, remembering the purpose of the discussion).

All these inter-related aspects of discussion can be modelled, discussed and practised in parallel, given appropriate materials and tasks.

See also in the key skills: Communication key skills level 2
Part A: In discussions...
          In giving a short talk...
Part B: C2.1a, C2.1b

Listen and respond

SLlr/L2

LEVEL 2 *At this level, adults can*

listen and respond
to spoken language, including extended information and narratives, and follow detailed explanations and multi-step instructions of varying length, adapting response to speaker, medium and context

speak to communicate
straightforward and detailed information, ideas and opinions clearly, adapting speech and content to take account of the listener(s), medium, purpose and situation

engage in discussion
with one or more people in a variety of different situations, making clear and effective contributions that produce outcomes appropriate to purpose and topic

in a wide range of formal and social exchanges

Skills, knowledge and understanding

Adults should be taught to:

❶ listen for and identify relevant information from extended explanations or presentations on a range of topics

– understand that relevance will depend on listening purpose

– know how to record key relevant points when listening over a more extended period

❷ listen to, understand and follow lengthy or multi-step instructions and narratives on a range of topics and in a range of contexts

– understand that different types of presentation make different demands on the listener (understanding and following step-by-step in sequence in instructions, reaching a cumulative understanding by the end of a narrative)

❸ respond to detailed or extended questions on a range of topics

– understand that some questions require the responder to address more than one sub-question or to give an extended answer that covers several points

– be able to construct coherent answers and keep track of the main thread when dealing with this type of question

Example

Listen to a presentation and note down key relevant points, e.g. from talk by a careers officer on training and employment opportunities in the area.

Follow and carry out instructions, e.g. from a supervisor recorded on a dictaphone.

Listen for pleasure to a short story, episode of a novel, autobiographical/travel account read aloud on the radio or on tape.

Speak at some length in response to open, evaluative questions, e.g. in a job review/appraisal/job counselling interview.

Sample activities

- Using a factual video of relevance to learners (e.g. from an education programme, training video), each person in a pair chooses/is allocated a particular aspect of the topic to listen for and to make a note of. After listening, pool findings, check understanding and discuss how particular aspects were introduced by the speaker. Listen again, this time focusing particularly on cues and signals related to their own aspect of the topic.

- Prepare for a presentation by an outside visitor, ideally in response to a need/interest expressed by the group (e.g. from a local volunteer bureau, training provider, social services department). In a group, consider the topic beforehand; each individual identifies how it might be relevant to them. Pose some specific questions people would like the presentation to answer and make a list of these on a flipchart; revise note-making strategies. Use the questions to help guide listening on the day, and make note of key points; use the list for asking follow-up questions after the presentation. Discuss information obtained and how to make use of it.

- Visit news web site (e.g. BBC News) and follow a video report of , for example, Budget details. Check understanding with other learners.

- In a group, explore the difference between following multi-step instructions that are written down and read and those that are listened to, e.g. how to remember, how to follow at the same time when listening, whether there are opportunities to re-cap and ask questions (on tape, or face to face with speaker). Practise following longer sets of instructions in different contexts, e.g.: watch a live step-by-step demonstration of a first aid procedure and carry it out; watch a craft demonstration on video, take some notes then make the same thing; listen to a simulated office message and write a memo to a named person, including particular details and information found; follow instructions from a recorded telephone information system.

- Listen to and discuss a range of narratives, live and recorded, for pleasure (making use of any community festival/educational storytelling events, local 'writers in residence' schemes, inviting elderly residents to relate tales of the neighbourhood, etc.), e.g. a 'sting in the tail' story, a suspense narrative, a hair-raising personal experience, a myth or legend. Consider how the experience of being read to and listening is different from both reading and watching narratives. Investigate taped stories for loan from local libraries.

- Identify more detailed or extended question types (e.g. open questions about more complex information, opinions and feelings). Discuss the listening and speaking skills for coping with these satisfactorily (e.g. recognising main focus of question, allowing oneself time to think before starting to speak, answering systematically, summing up). As a group, identify some questions for a survey (e.g. related to people's experience, skills, preferences, ambitions for areas of employment or training) which will require people to answer reflectively and at some length. In pairs, survey each other and tape the responses, to use both to judge own responses and to keep as record of own views and feelings.

- Prepare and hold an *Any Questions* session, allocating roles to each person (can use well-known real people or 'personas', e.g. Swampy or 'a passionate environmentalist and anti-road campaigner'). Devise some extended questions which will seek out the opinions of the panel. Give people a week to think about the sort of answers they will give. With teacher as chairperson, divide into panel and questioners; then reverse so that each person is panel member at some point. Teacher observes answering techniques and leads post-mortem discussion on giving focused answers on large or detailed subjects.

See also in the key skills:

Communication key skills level 2
Part A: In discussions...
        In giving a short talk...
Part B: C2.1a, C2.1b

LEVEL 2

At this level, adults can

listen and respond
to spoken language, including extended information and narratives, and follow detailed explanations and multi-step instructions of varying length, adapting response to speaker, medium and context

speak to communicate
straightforward and detailed information, ideas and opinions clearly, adapting speech and content to take account of the listener(s), medium, purpose and situation

engage in discussion
with one or more people in a variety of different situations, making clear and effective contributions that produce outcomes appropriate to purpose and topic

in a wide range of formal and social exchanges

Listen and respond

SLlr/L2

Skills, knowledge and understanding

Adults should be taught to:

4 respond to criticism and criticise constructively

– understand that successful co-operation involves people being able to deal with and offer criticism in constructive ways, in order to agree the best solution

– know and apply strategies for listening and speaking with care when exchanging opinions and judgements

Example

Successfully handle a delicate situation in a work/community or educational context which involves people passing judgement on others' actions/opinions/ideas, e.g. on whether a local building should be used as a bail hostel.

Speak to communicate

SLc/L2

Skills, knowledge and understanding

Adults should be taught to:

1 speak clearly and confidently in a way which suits the situation

– know how to adapt the way of speaking (pace, volume, articulation) to suit listener, context and purpose

– be able to sustain a clear, confident and appropriate style in formal and social exchanges of varying length

Example

Give a talk or presentation to other learners.

Present information in a meeting, e.g. at work, a union meeting, a public meeting about a local issue, parents' meeting.

2 make requests and ask questions to obtain detailed information in familiar and unfamiliar contexts

– understand that to get detailed information involves wording questions carefully, asking follow-up ones to probe further if necessary

Ask for information on an unfamiliar subject requiring precise details (e.g. how, when and where to register a birth, marriage or death, what papers to supply, what signatures, etc.).

Sample activities

- Explore what the group thinks is legitimate criticism of others and what is not, in terms of context, topic, aspect, how expressed. Discuss why people might find criticism hard to take, the reactions criticism can provoke, the dangers to avoid when criticising others' behaviour, ideas, etc. Explore where criticism might be constructive and necessary, and the drawbacks of no one daring to disagree with anyone else. Discuss how and why constructive criticism is about effective speaking and listening. Draw up and display some agreed ground rules for offering and responding to criticism in the group.

- Watch some training video clips of constructive criticism in a one-to-one, team or group context and identify the sorts of language and non-verbal signals that make it acceptable when offered; add them to the ground rules (e.g. non-aggressive tone of voice, non-threatening use of person's name, receptive rather than hostile body language, open facial expression). Add rules for accepting criticism appropriately, e.g. not going on the defensive, accepting it if it is fair *(OK, I'll admit I made a mess of that ...)*, responding calmly and constructively if it feels unfair (e.g. *I can see it might look like that but actually ...).* Try to apply all these ground rules in real situations in the group, and beyond.

Sample activities

- Prepare for, plan and deliver a talk to fellow learners. Watch a model presentation on video and discuss key elements: structure, organisation and presentation of content, choice of vocabulary and phrasing, clarity and tone of voice, variety of pace, emphasis, use of humour, etc. In a group, devise a feedback evaluation sheet for reporting on a presentation. As individuals, using a topic of interest or related to other curriculum/training activities, identify information/material to be conveyed; make notes to sequence points; decide on the method of presentation and prepare. Discuss issues of delivery, e.g. location, audience, equipment available, etc. Give talk to other group members who each complete an evaluation sheet. Discuss these with teacher.

- Take part in a short debate, ideally with own group and another group. Study main conventions of debating via video clips. Select an issue of interest; choose which side to speak on and, with others on that side, research, plan and prepare two speeches for proposer and seconder plus supplementary points for follow-up to other side's speeches. All practise delivering speeches, taking turns to act as observers/coaches and prepare delivery of supplementary points, deciding who will be responsible for saying what. Hold debate chaired by teacher. Evaluate collectively at the end: how clear, interesting and entertaining were all the contributions?

- Take part in a group visit to a library/information centre (college, work place or public library) where the purpose is to find out about what facilities are available for users. As a group, identify some questions beforehand (e.g. re Internet access, local directories, community or employment or consumer information; specialist magazines; loan services: books, videos, tapes, CDs, CD Roms, pictures; how to join; any charges). Decide which pairs will be responsible for finding out how to access which information. Prepare questions beforehand and consider how to record answers (e.g. notes, picking up leaflets, photocopying). After the visit share feedback on the process of finding out and any lessons learnt; use information obtained as subject of pair presentations to group/other classes.

See also in the key skills:

Communication key skills level 2
Part A: In discussions...
          In giving a short talk...
Part B: C2.1a, C2.1b

LEVEL 2 *At this level, adults can*

listen and respond
to spoken language, including extended information and narratives, and follow detailed explanations and multi-step instructions of varying length, adapting response to speaker, medium and context

speak to communicate
straightforward and detailed information, ideas and opinions clearly, adapting speech and content to take account of the listener(s), medium, purpose and situation

engage in discussion
with one or more people in a variety of different situations, making clear and effective contributions that produce outcomes appropriate to purpose and topic

in a wide range of formal and social exchanges

Speak to communicate   SLc/L2

Skills, knowledge and understanding

Adults should be taught to:

3 express clearly statements of fact, explanations, instructions, accounts, descriptions using appropriate structure, style and vocabulary

– know and use an appropriate range of vocabulary and syntax in order to communicate more complex meanings

– adapt the level of formality in language and style depending on the situation and listeners

– know how to structure what is said, using markers which help listeners to follow the line of thought

Example

Put forward a proposal, e.g. at a parents' meeting, union or party political meeting.

4 present information and ideas in a logical sequence and provide further detail and development to clarify or confirm understanding

– understand that when giving information orally speakers can invite listeners to clarify their understanding as they go along

– know how to structure main points, expand on information, and be able to respond to listeners' queries while maintaining the logical thread of ideas

Present some information to other learners (e.g. researched from a housing association, childcare provider, council one-stop shop), dealing with questions in the course of the talk.

Engage in discussion   SLd/L2

In this section, it is expected that elements from both **Listen and respond** and **Speak to communicate** will be used as well as those shown below

Skills, knowledge and understanding

Adults should be taught to:

1 make relevant contributions and help to move discussions forward

– understand that, to be productive, discussion needs to progress towards agreed decisions, proposals and solutions

– know how to prevent discussion getting bogged down, by making constructive contributions and interventions

Example

Take part in a discussion to make decisions on a difficult topic (e.g. union negotiations on pay and conditions, community/tenants' association policy on allowing alcohol/drug addicts access to local facilities).

Sample activities

- Watch/listen to some clips of people speaking (e.g. explaining or describing an aspect of a specialist subject, arguing a case, persuading people to a particular viewpoint); analyse the vocabulary (e.g. any technical terms, persuasive language, formal terms of address). Listen again for distinctive turns of phrase, emphasis, repetition, and signals which link points together (e.g. *firstly, secondly, finally, on the one hand, on the other, whereas, nevertheless, even so, however, therefore*). In pairs, decide on a topic on which to plan and present a short account, explanation, description (e.g. a hobby or shared interest; something both feel strongly about); organise points, identify any specialist vocabulary which might need explaining, plan to make points alternately, deciding on how each one will round off a point and how the other will pick up the next one. Present the talk, bringing it to an apt conclusion.

- Practise adapting talk to context by playing 'On The Spot'. Each person draws out a situation from a hat and prepares to speak for at least a minute on it (e.g. explain to a child how to use a pelican crossing; give set of instructions for a new learner on registering at the resources centre; welcome an outside speaker to the group; persuade a colleague to contribute to a fundraising event; protest to centre head on behalf of group against an unpopular decision). Discuss differences of style, structure and vocabulary which the contributions employ.

- Listen to some sample presentations of information or ideas, some good and some bad (from a training video, or constructed for the occasion). Identify features of language and organisation which make some easier to follow than others (e.g. defining technical language, thinking about what people need to be told before they can understand the significance of something else, signalling how one point is linked to the next, reminding listeners of the main thread after answering a specific question, clarifying a point by explaining it again in a different way, resisting the temptation to wander off at a tangent or go into too much detail when replying to requests for clarification). Draw up a list of 'good practice' points for display.

- Try out the good practice guidelines in the context of practising how to make a complaint about a product or service, supporting case with details. In groups of three, using a given context or own experience, take turns to make the complaint, question the complainant, and to observe; tape the exchanges. Afterwards evaluate how well the case was presented, information sequenced and supported, questions dealt with and main thread maintained.

- Use a text-to-speech program to attach voice footnotes to a complex text, e.g. an assignment for an NVQ or A level course.

Sample activities

- Re-cap on what makes effective discussion, then watch a training video clip and note how speakers move the discussion forward (e.g. making constructive points, picking up and developing others' points, summarising, reminding people why they are having the discussion to re-focus on purpose). Discuss observations, identify how constructive discussion involves careful listening as well as speaking. Watch again to note particularly effective participants. Draw up some tips for achieving useful outcomes from discussion.

- Investigate how discussions can be opened, re-capped and concluded (e.g. *OK, I'll start things off; Let's just check where we've got to…/ Can we just recap so far…?/So are we nearly there? I'm not sure whether we've decided anything yet…/Anyone want to say anything else…?/Does everyone know what they're doing…?*). Identify advantages and disadvantages of having someone chair a discussion and what the role of a chairperson might be (e.g. to introduce issues, encourage fair spread of contributions, re-cap, sum up, etc.). Watch some video clips of chaired discussions. Plan and hold a group discussion where a decision is required (e.g. take roles to discuss the possible future of an adult education centre faced with closure) and experiment with and without a chairperson.

See also in the key skills:

Communication key skills level 2
Part A: In discussions...
     In giving a short talk...
Part B: C2.1a, C2.1b

LEVEL 2 *At this level, adults can*

listen and respond
to spoken language, including extended information and narratives, and follow detailed explanations and multi-step instructions of varying length, adapting response to speaker, medium and context

speak to communicate
straightforward and detailed information, ideas and opinions clearly, adapting speech and content to take account of the listener(s), medium, purpose and situation

engage in discussion
with one or more people in a variety of different situations, making clear and effective contributions that produce outcomes appropriate to purpose and topic

in a wide range of formal and social exchanges

Engage in discussion

SLd/L2

Skills, knowledge and understanding

Adults should be taught to:

2 **adapt contributions to discussions to suit audience, context, purpose and situation**

– understand that what makes contributions appropriate will vary depending on what hinges on the discussion, the make-up of the group, the degree of urgency, etc.

– be able to adapt own contributions in terms of number, length, level of detail to suit different circumstances

3 **use appropriate phrases for interruption and change of topic**

– know how to signal an intervention and how to change the topic when appropriate, without dominating the discussion

4 **support opinions and arguments with evidence**

– understand that productive discussion involves making valid and convincing points, not browbeating people to accept own view

– know how to research information for a discussion

– use factual information and knowledge to support views and arguments

5 **use strategies intended to reassure (e.g. body language and appropriate phraseology)**

– understand that productive discussion involves trust and co-operation, which allow differences to be aired constructively

– know and use gestures and phrases which signal co-operation and respect for group

Example

Make useful contributions to different discussions with staff and other learners, e.g. quickly decide how to complete an activity there and then, meet with representatives from different classes to decide and plan events for Adult Learners Week.

Make own points and help discussion cover necessary ground in a meeting to decide on a course of action, e.g. whether to wind up a local club/team/association which is struggling to get participants.

Put forward a well-supported point at a meeting (e.g. of a parents' association, pressure group, as a representative of an interest group, such as union, claimants, residents).

Take part in a heated discussion which remains good-natured and productive (e.g. to decide and plan a group outing or event).

Sample activities

- Identify different purposes for discussions in the learning context and elsewhere (e.g. quickly deciding who is doing what in a group, taking longer to plan something more complicated or to consider how to deal with a significant problem). Think about the types of contribution appropriate in different contexts (e.g. practical suggestions, useful information, reminders, reflective observations, exploratory *what if*s, etc.). Make a chart/list of types of contribution related to purpose to reinforce importance of using the time most effectively.

- Practise taking part in a range of discussions with different contexts and purposes (e.g. a short group activity, a group project over time, a 'what next' discussion with learners on same course from another centre; investigate an issue with representatives of outside bodies – if possible, via a video conferencing link with adult learners in another area). Gain experience of taking different roles (e.g. chair, note taker, observer). Evaluate contributions for how well they help discussion fulfil its purpose.

- Recap on useful tactics for taking opportunities to interrupt and make a point (choosing the moment, using previous speaker's point as lead-in for own, using body language to signal wish to speak, etc.). Consider how to develop these to shift discussion topic when progress is not being made. Watch some video clips and observe strategies and phrases. Make a list of useful 'moving on' phrases (e.g. *We seem to have gone round this one a few times – how about looking at…?/Moving on from that, shall we…?/It might be worth considering…/ I suggest we think about…/What about the issue of…/Don't let's forget…/ We haven't mentioned… There's still the matter of…*, etc.).

- Evaluate how good the group is at using these strategies. When next having a discussion to sort something out, appoint an observer to comment on whether the discussion loses its way at any point and how well members of the group manage to turn it in a useful direction.

- Study video training clips to identify the difference between convincing people and wearing them down. Drawing on own experience, discuss implications of people 'agreeing' with others without being convinced. Identify the sorts of discussion where use of reliable evidence is particularly important (e.g. when trying to arrive at a decision that will have consequences for others). Make a list of *do*s and *don't*s for making well-supported points (e.g. DO: refer to at least one example/fact/statistic, consider general implications of a particular point; DON'T: use loud voice or aggressive mannerisms to try to persuade listeners, hector, keep repeating same point in hope of convincing eventually).

- Use 'mini case studies' to raise awareness of the difference between assertion and supported points. Group is given a situation to look at from various standpoints, each person representing one; people have five minutes to decide on points they want to make. Use teacher as observer to evaluate how well people use evidence in support of their views. Discuss tactics that convince and those that irritate/provoke opposition.

- Use this experience to hold an extended discussion for which people research information beforehand to use as supporting evidence.

- Consider differences between discussion with familiar people and with strangers/acquaintances who won't know what to expect. Identify reassuring behaviour (e.g. smiling, sitting back in chair, paying attention to other speakers, confirming other speakers' points, etc.); also consider language which conveys reassurance and sounds genuine, while still expressing disagreement if necessary (e.g. *I think Nazeen's idea is a good one because…/If it's OK with the group, I'd like to suggest…/I know this may sound like a wild idea, but I wonder whether…/Sorry, Chris, but I'm going to have to disagree with that, because…/I'd like to put forward another view on that, Mrs Brown, if I may…*, etc.).

- Video own group discussion on a contentious issue and play back to look for instances of reassurance in body language and phraseology, stopping to invite comment and observations. Discuss how these features interact with other discussion skills, such as turn taking, phrases for interruption and topic changing, using evidence to convince, careful listening and relevant response, etc.

Reading

Reading matters

The ability to read is as important today as it ever was. Some people believe that the need for good basic skills has lessened as technology has improved, that television, with all its power and indeed its role in providing information, has reduced the need for reading. Certainly there are many people who don't buy books for pleasure and enjoyment, and some who rarely read a newspaper or visit a library. In some ways this may not really matter. Being able to read fluently is very different from wanting to read at all. In so many aspects of our life we still *need* to read, a need technology cannot replace. Indeed in some ways it makes it more essential. As more everyday activities become automated, so reading becomes more important.

> 'It's awful when your grandson says to you "read me a story, grandad", and you can't do it. You always want to get out of it – "I'm busy, I'm doing something". You always want to make an excuse.'

from *A Fresh Start – Improving Literacy and Numeracy*, DFEE, 1999

Texts

The choice of texts used to develop reading skills at each level is crucial. The key is to use a variety of texts whose type and purpose cover the range identified in the standard, even though they will necessarily be in simplified form at lower levels. What learners do with texts must be both meaningful in terms of helping them achieve the standard and in helping them become effective learners. The texts used must include those relevant to the interests of the individual, but there must also be texts that enable the learner to apply new skills in new contexts – effectively to develop transferable skills. If this doesn't happen, they won't get any better at coping with literacy demands, because there won't be the cumulative learning that results in 'great leaps forward'.

> Some books are to be tasted, others to be swallowed, and some few to be chewed and digested: that is, some books are to be read only in parts; others to be read, but not curiously; and some few to be read wholly and with diligence and attention.

Francis Bacon, 1561–1626

At this level, adults can

read and understand
short texts with repeated language patterns on familiar topics

read and obtain information
from common signs and symbols

in texts such as public signs and notices, lists, forms, records, simple narratives

---

Skills, knowledge and understanding

Adults should be taught to:

❶ follow a short narrative on a familiar topic or experience

– know that text on a page goes from left to right and from top to bottom and be able to track a simple text as they read it aloud for themselves

– know and use a range of text-level strategies to get at meaning: their own background knowledge of content, the context of the text as a whole, presentational devices

– know that it is not always necessary to read every word in order to comprehend or gain information from a text

– understand that texts can be sources of information and enjoyment

– know some basic metalanguage that distinguishes written text from spoken texts, e.g. *text, page, format, layout, print, image, caption, line, title, sentence, word, letter*

❷ recognise the different purposes of texts at this level

– understand that different types of text will look different and that the format can often help identify the purpose of texts

– know that symbols without words have meaning and understand the meaning of common signs and symbols

Example

Read their own composition, which someone else has written down.

Predict a text's likely subject matter from information on the title page, or the headline of a newspaper article, and judge if it will be of use or interest to themselves.

Recognise the purpose of simple texts encountered in daily life, e.g. a greetings card, an advert, a notice, an appointment card, a shopping list, a road sign.

Recognise and understand the signs for No Smoking, Ladies, Gents, EXIT, ENTRANCE, Bus Stop.

Skills, knowledge and understanding

Adults should be taught to:

❶ read and recognise simple sentence structures

– know that language is rule governed and understand that word order affects meaning

– use implicit knowledge of language rules to predict meaning and check for sense

– understand the concept of a sentence

– know the name and understand the function of a full stop and an initial capital letter in a sentence and apply this knowledge to help with reading

– understand that not all texts consist of whole sentences

– know that, as well as marking a new sentence, capital letters are used for names and places and for the personal pronoun 'I'

Example

Read simple sentences and check for sense, e.g.

My name is Maria. I have two children.

Point the spray away from your face. Now press the top.

Sample activities

- Practise tracking the order of print through simple texts of different types, as someone else reads them aloud.

- Track texts in supported reading.

- Answer questions about a text by looking at a labelled diagram.

- Look at the headlines on Ceefax (p. 101) or Oracle (p. 300) and choose the most interesting story (e.g. *Bush wins by 327 votes*).

Language experience

Use texts prepared by the learners themselves. The language and content will be familiar to them. Texts can be recorded on tape by the learner for transcription, or dictated to the teacher.

- Explain the purpose of different short texts.
- Sort different short texts into categories of purpose.
- Make a collection of short texts from home, work or leisure, and discuss their purpose and relevance.
- Explain workplace signs and symbols to a colleague or teacher.
- Match symbols of household products to their meaning.
- Use knowledge of context and presentation to work out the meaning of signs encountered in their daily life.

Sample activities

- Discuss the concept of sentence with their teacher using their own language-experience text.
- Highlight or underline the initial letter of sentences and full stops in simple sentences in a short text on paper or screen.
- Highlight separate sentences in different colours in a short text.
- Use a wordprocessor to break a text into sentences.
- Highlight: the upper-case letters in their own personal details; the pronoun 'I' in a simple text.
- Using a word processor, put full stops in a passage of language experience.

ENTRY
1
LEVEL

At this level, adults can

read and understand
short texts with repeated language patterns on familiar topics

read and obtain information
from common signs and symbols

in texts such as public signs and notices, lists, forms, records, simple narratives

Word Focus   Vocabulary, word recognition and phonics   Rw/E1

Skills, knowledge and understanding

Adults should be taught to:

❶ possess a limited, meaningful sight vocabulary of words, signs and symbols

– understand that written words carry meaning and that adults will already be familiar with many of the words they will meet in print, from their experience of spoken language

– understand that some words occur in texts more frequently than others and recognise key high-frequency words

– understand that there are words which are key personal words for them and their situation, identify these words and learn to recognise them

– know and apply some techniques for recognising words on sight: length, shape, initial letter combinations, association with other words

❷ decode simple, regular words

– understand that own language experience can be used when reading, to help predict sense and meaning of words

– understand that illustrations and other graphics can give clues to the likely meaning of individual words

– understand that written words correspond to their spoken equivalents and are composed of letters in combinations, to represent spoken sounds

– identify sounds in familiar regular words from spoken experience and recognise correspondence between sounds (phonemes) and letters (graphemes)

❸ recognise the letters of the alphabet in both upper and lower case

– understand that letters can be represented in different ways, e.g. upper and lower case, different fonts and sizes

– know that letters of the alphabet occur in a particular sequence

– recognise, sound, name and sequence the letters of the alphabet

– understand and use the terms *vowel* and *consonant*

Example

Social sight vocabulary.

Key words from Dolch list.

Recognise phoneme–grapheme correspondence in: initial consonant letter sounds; short vowel sounds, initial consonant clusters, final consonant clusters (see Writing curriculum, p.107).

Read and understand a very simple text in sentences, based on familiar words and simple regular words, e.g. some facts about own life written down by someone else.

Recognise the same sign in upper and lower case.

Find a personal key word in their own list.

Sample activities

- Highlight their own name/street/town/ city in a list.
- Draw an outline around personal key words to identify word shape and trace with their finger.
- Highlight key words from their personal list in their own composition which someone else has written down.
- Match personal key words by playing 'Snap'.
- Highlight the days of the week in familiar material such as a newspaper, TV listings.
- Find ways of remembering common words, e.g. pinning them up at home.
- Use a text-to-speech program to check accurate reading of key vocabulary list, stored in a Word document.

- Develop phonemic awareness, e.g. by listening to, learning and reciting the words of raps, jingles or sound poems and exploring rhyme, alliteration and other sound patterns.
- Insert vowels into gaps at the beginning or middle of simple words, e.g. *bet, in, at, cot.*
- Play missing vowel sound or initial/final consonant cluster bingo.
- Highlight consonant clusters in a short piece of text.
- Listen to a tape of sentences, each containing a repeated key word. On an accompanying written text, identify phonemes in repeated word, e.g. The **shop** is open – sh/o/p.
- Practise reading some very simple illustrated, customised texts, some made up of sentences, based on simple regular words and familiar sight vocabulary. Use knowledge of sound–letter correspondences, plus context, grammatical and textual clues to get at meaning. Discuss process with teacher.

Miscellaneous words from social sight vocabulary

on	high	bottom
off	low	this way up
salt	shampoo	careful
sugar	poison	fragile
tea	cleaner	open here
coffee	days of the week	open other side
front	months of the year	handle with care
back	year	urgent
left	parcels	
right	top	

Important words in learning to read (from the Dolch list)

a	other	her	said
I	night	into	we
it	some	little	about
the	then	make	been
all	two	much	by
be	well	no	can
for	what	off	did
his	which	or	first
on	and	out	go
so	in	see	here
with	of	their	just
an	to	there	look
before	as	up	more
call	but	went	must
come	had	when	new
do	him	will	old
from	one	your	our
has	they	he	over
if	you	is	she
like	back	that	them
made	big	was	this
me	came	at	want
my	could	are	were
now	down	have	where
only	get	not	who

- Compare the presentation of written signs around them in upper and lower case and recognise that they represent the same words.
- Match words in different fonts and styles, e.g. *Ford* to FORD; *No Parking* to NO PARKING.
- Highlight the same letters printed in a variety of sizes and fonts in a newspaper.
- Sort letters into alphabetical order.
- Arrange a list of common/personal/topic key words in alphabetical order, using the initial letter, which when written out could serve as a reference list for their own writing.
- Use the CAPS LOCK key to recognise upper- and lower-case letters in different fonts, including TIMES NEW ROMAN (serif) and ARIAL (sans serif).
- Use the keypad on a mobile phone to find and input first and second names.

At this level,
adults can

read and understand
short texts with repeated
language patterns on familiar
topics

read and obtain information
from common signs and symbols

in texts such as public signs and
notices, lists, forms, records,
simple narratives

An example of an integrated activity for reading   E1

Teaching focus

Text: some conventions and purposes of simple written texts

Sentence: the concept of a sentence, of full stops and initial capitals and of capital *I*

Word: written words as carriers of meaning and their relationship to words already known in speech; initial consonant sounds and sound–letter correspondence

Myself

My name is Ann Lao. I have two sisters and one brother. My brother lives in Hull. I have a little boy called Mark. He is two years old. He is learning to talk. I want to get better at reading and writing. I want to help Mark. I really want to do that!

The reading text is one of several arising from conversation between a small group of learners and their teacher, about themselves and their reasons for attending classes. The teacher has created a text for Ann by adapting her talk into written language organised in sentences. The group has discussed the relationship between speech and writing: that written words carry the same meaning as their spoken equivalents, that words in writing are usually arranged in sentences. So the teacher has had to adapt what the group has told her to turn each person's spoken account into a written text.

- Give each learner their word-processed text (the teacher has a large-print version of all of them). Read out each text to the group, checking that details are correct and the subjects are happy with them.

- In pairs, learners look at both their texts together to spot any similarities, and highlight them; these might be title, capital letters, full stops, some common words. Pool findings and mark up on the large-print versions so everyone can see similarities between all the texts and can discuss them. Introduce/reinforce the relevant terms and their functions, writing them up for display: *text, title, letter, capital letter, capital I, full stop, sentence.*

- Write up all the shared words, asking the group to consider why some words came up in all or most people's texts. (Games and self-study tasks can be used later to reinforce knowledge of these shared sight words.)

- Read each person's text individually to them, asking them to follow it and identify any words they recognise. Discuss these words and their significance for the reader and start off an individual dictionary for each person. (Reinforcement activities for learning personal key words can be set for later self-study.) For Ann's text, discussion could cover initial capitals for names of people and places: *Ann, Mark, Hull*; the words *brother, sisters, reading, writing* (including concept of a silent letter); the exclamation mark to show her strong feeling which came over when she spoke about the importance of Mark to her and to her motivation; the repetition of sentences beginning with *I* because the text is about herself.

- Meanwhile, ask all learners to identify and highlight words that share the same initial letters in their texts, e.g. (in Ann's text) *have, help, he, Hull; little, learning, lives, Lao; brother, boy, better.* Ask the group to share findings and identify which letters they know the name and/or sound of. (This can tie in with detailed work on the alphabet and initial letter–sound correspondence, which can be reinforced with sound games, raps, exercises, self-study work collecting jingles, advertising slogans, etc.).

- Ask the group to look again at their texts. What is the difference between having this information about themselves written down as opposed to just in their own heads? What purpose do these texts serve? Why give a text a title? How might these texts be developed later, and what title might they have? Give each person a clean copy of their text to add to their personal file along with the worked version.

Links with speaking, listening and discussion

Such texts for reading grow out of exchanges between the teacher and the learners, and provide opportunity for making statements of fact clearly. Learners must work with each other, using simple exchanges in the context of completing a task.

Links with writing

Reading texts about the self models the content, typical sentence structure and vocabulary of simple autobiographical texts. Learners can begin to extend texts produced by their teacher by composing additional sentences in a similar pattern and writing them down for themselves, with help as necessary. Filing all such work will build up an autobiographical text that can be re-visited and elaborated as learners' writing skills develop.

ENTRY LEVEL 2 *At this level, adults can*

read and understand
short, straightforward texts on familiar topics

read and obtain information
from short documents, familiar sources and signs and symbols

in texts such as public signs and notices, lists, forms, notes, records, e-mails, simple narratives, letters and diagrams

| Text Focus | **Reading comprehension** | **Rt/E2** |

Skills, knowledge and understanding

Adults should be taught to:

❶ trace and understand the main events of chronological and instructional texts

– understand that chronological text is related to events in time

– understand that instructional texts must be read in sequence

– know and use text-level strategies to predict content and check meaning, e.g. their own background knowledge, context of text as a whole, title, headings, illustrations

❷ recognise the different purposes of texts at this level

– understand that different texts have different purposes, e.g. to explain, inform, instruct, entertain

❸ identify common sources of information

– understand that different sources of information are designed for different uses, e.g. newspaper, directory, listing

– understand that similar information can be found in different sources and be presented in different ways

– understand that sources can be electronic as well as paper based, e.g. teletext, web sites

– understand that reading for information often involves locating specific details rather than reading a whole text

❹ use illustrations and captions to locate information

– understand that illustrations contribute to meaning and can help locate and interpret information

Example

Read a short story to a child.

Follow a simple set of instructions in labelled pictures.

Know the different purposes of texts encountered in daily life, e.g. personal letters, junk mail, invoices, TV listings, DIY manuals, recipes, magazine stories, tickets for an event.

Know where to find out what is on television (i.e. newspaper, TV guide, teletext).

Use an illustration to check progress in following a set of instructions.

Sample activities

- Put pictures and sentences in the correct sequence and read the completed account.
- Read simple recounts and note features, e.g. sequenced events, use of words such as *first, next, after, when*.
- Sequence a set of instructions so they can be carried out, e.g. taking medicines, following a basic recipe, cleaning paintbrushes.
- Sort a range of texts into instructional texts and others and note the key structural features of instructions, e.g. clear statement of purpose; set of steps in sequence, often numbered; direct language.

- Discuss the purpose of different short texts and identify features that characterise the text type.
- Sort different texts into categories of purpose, e.g. letters, instructions, stories, adverts.
- Select their own reading for pleasure from a range of material at this level; read and discuss texts with fellow learners and teacher.

- Sort and match information to its source, e.g. football results to newspaper sports section, definitions of words to dictionary, list of dentists to Yellow Pages.
- Identify a personal list of information needs and likely sources as a checklist for learning and use.
- Use the front page of a web site (e.g. MSN, AOL) to find items of news, sport, gossip, entertainment.

- Match statements to illustrations, e.g. newspaper headlines to photographs.
- Choose a subject of use or interest and identify some information required. Choose a suitable text and use the illustrations as a guide to where in the text the information is likely to be. Check if it is there.
- Match common icons to their meaning and/or purpose (e.g. *save, cut, paste*).

| Sentence Focus | **Grammar and punctuation** | **Rs/E2** |

Skills, knowledge and understanding

Adults should be taught to:

❶ read and understand linking words and adverbials in instructions and directions (e.g. *next, then, right* and *straight on*)

  – understand that these types of word and phrase: expand the information in a sentence by providing details about place, sequence, time; relate one step of the instructions/directions to another, enabling the reader to follow the whole text and complete the task

❷ use knowledge of simple sentence structure and word order to help decipher unfamiliar words and predict meaning

  – understand that sentences follow grammatical patterns, and certain types of words are more likely to occur in some places than others

  – understand that word order and the relationship between words in a sentence are as important to meaning as the words themselves

❸ apply own life experience and knowledge to check out plausible meanings of a sentence as a whole when decoding unfamiliar words

  – understand that an unknown word must make sense in the context of the complete sentence, and that this will rule out most alternatives

❹ use punctuation and capitalisation to aid understanding

  – understand that different punctuation marks are used for different purposes and know their names: *full stop, question* and *exclamation marks* for end of sentence

  – understand that this punctuation serves to help the reader make sense of written text, and apply this understanding in their own reading

  – understand that all end-of-sentence markers are followed by an initial capital in continuous text written in complete sentences

Example

Use the information in adverbials and linking words to help follow a sequence of written instructions or directions.

Make general sense of a simple continuous text written in sentences, encountered in daily life, even if they are not able to read every word.

Check out possible plausible meanings in their own reading, e.g. in a sentence in a letter.

Recognise and take account of full stops, question marks, exclamation marks in their own reading.

Sample activities

- Highlight on paper or screen words and phrases in texts that link sentences, and provide details about sequence, time and place, e.g. *after, before, then, next, during, meanwhile, after a while, to one side, next to, right, left, straight on.*

- Follow simple written directions to get from one place to another.

- Put jumbled instructions into a logical order, where it is necessary to use the linking words to determine the order.

- Complete a cloze exercise (selecting words to fill gaps) on paper or screen, on a simple continuous text in sentences, where only a certain type of word (e.g. noun, verb, preposition, adverbial, adjective) will make grammatical sense in that position, and only certain meanings are possible in each instance. Select the right word for each gap (from a list provided, if necessary). Read the complete text to check for sense, replacing any words that clearly do not fit.

- Read and re-order words in sentences in familiar texts, including their own writing, and assess the effect on meaning, e.g. *My name is Frank. Frank is my name. Is my name Frank?*

- Apply a cloze program (e.g. *Developing Tray*, tool in *SkillsBuild*) to a simple text, leaving the words visible for the learner to insert.

- Raise awareness of the the relevance of experience and knowledge in helping make sense of words in sentences by reading some extracts from different types of text where more than one word is offered in certain places. Decide which word will fit and discuss with partner how they know this to be the case, e.g. with *The walker/water went on up the hill.* the word cannot be *water*, which does not go uphill.

- Highlight full stops, question marks and exclamation marks in simple texts. Read the whole text and discuss the effect of having these punctuation marks where they are.

- Read aloud with correct intonation and pauses, if appropriate for their own reading plan.

At this level,
adults can

read and understand
short, straightforward texts on
familiar topics

read and obtain information
from short documents, familiar
sources and signs and symbols

in texts such as public signs and
notices, lists, forms, notes,
records, e-mails, simple
narratives, letters and diagrams

| Word Focus | Vocabulary, word recognition and phonics | Rw/E2 |

Skills, knowledge and understanding

Adults should be taught to:

❶ read and understand words on forms related to personal information (e.g. first name, surname, address, postcode, age, date of birth)

❷ recognise high-frequency words and words with common spelling patterns
  – read on sight high-frequency words
  – read on sight personal key words
  – know and use different techniques for learning to read words on sight, e.g. association, visual shape, and pattern context

❸ use phonic and graphic knowledge to decode words
  – understand that the meaning of individual words can often be deduced from surrounding context, using own life knowledge and experience as a guide
  – understand that knowledge of sound and letter correspondence can be applied alongside these contextual clues to help decode words, e.g. use of initial phonemes/letters
  – understand that the same sound (phoneme) can be spelt in more than one way and that the same spelling (grapheme) can represent more than one sound
  – reinforce and extend knowledge of sound–letter patterns in simple words with common spelling patterns
  – understand that some words can be split into specific parts, and recognise the parts, including compound words, prefixes, suffixes, inflectional endings, plurals, e.g. *playground, replay, playful, playing, played, plays*
  – understand how each beat in a word is a syllable and breaking some words into syllables can help to decode them, e.g. *family*

❹ use a simplified dictionary to find the meaning of unfamiliar words
  – understand the function of dictionaries
  – understand that dictionaries are organised alphabetically

❺ use initial letters to find and sequence words in alphabetical order
  – understand that you do not have to start at the beginning of a list/dictionary
  – use the initial letter to locate the starting point quickly

Example

Read and understand what personal information is needed to complete a form in a real-life task.

Social sight vocabulary for written signs.

High-frequency words from Dolch list.

Months of the year.

Read a simple text, using appropriate strategies to attempt every word.

Read words with common spelling patterns for long vowel phonemes:

ee (feet), ea (seat);

a–e (name), ay (play), ai (train);

ie (lie), i–e (bite), igh (high), y (fly);

oa (boat), o–e (pole) ow (show);

oo (moon), u–e (tune) ew (flew), ue (blue).

Read words with common spelling patterns for vowel phonemes:

oo – u (pull), oo (good);

ar – ar (car);

oy – oi (boil), oy (boy);

ow – ow (cow), ou (sound).

Find a word in a simplified dictionary.

Look up unknown words from their own reading in a simplified dictionary.

Sample activities

- Identify what personal information is asked for on a variety of forms relevant to their situation, e.g. prescription, car-tax renewal, mail-order form, loyalty-card application, etc.

- Find a simple registration form on a web site (one step from most search engines). Cut and paste into own file/copy.

- Read aloud flashcards of high-frequency words and their own familiar words.

- Play 'Snap' with high-frequency words/their own familiar words.

- Insert high-frequency words/their own familiar words into gaps in sentences.

- Sort lists of words on a card into groups according to spelling pattern.

- Match list of words with the same spelling pattern to their meanings, e.g.

  gar- garden, garbage, garlic

  You grow things in it.

- Find words in a text that have the same letter pattern as *–and.*

- Underline in different colours, on paper or on a word processor, words with two syllables, three syllables, and four syllables.

- Insert a space between syllables in a list of words on a computer by using the space bar.

- With a reading partner, practise reading skills on a selection of short extracts from texts with different purposes, e.g. from a letter, instructions, an advert, a notice, a story. Read an extract/text highlighting unknown words as encountered, but keep reading. At the end of each extract go back to the beginning and discuss the following questions: *What is the text for? Who is it aimed at? What is it about?* Then re-read, stopping at the highlighted words. Discuss what would fit the sense. Apply some word-level strategies as appropriate, e.g.: *What is the initial sound? What are the possible vowel sounds? Can it be divided into syllables/free-standing parts? Is any part of the word recognisable?*, etc. Agree the likely reading. Re-read the whole sentence to check for sense. When all highlighted words have been attempted, re-read the whole extract/text to the teacher; discuss the process of arriving at meaning, including how any misunderstandings came about.

- Put lists of words into alphabetical order using the computer.

- Put names of family members in the correct alphabetical order.

- Find their own name in a class list.

- Practise opening a dictionary at the approximate point where the initial letter is to be found.

- Practise looking up known words in a dictionary as quickly as possible.

- Look up unknown words from their own reading in a simplified dictionary and use the word in their own sentence.

- Put a simple list (e.g. of names, occupations, colours) in order in a Word table. Check answer by using the functions 'Table: Sort'.

'Sign' words from social sight vocabulary

for sale	wash	private	pull
lifts	brush up	toilets	saloon
bus	hot	closed	bar
wet paint	cold	open	way out
lunch	beware of the dog	push	telephone

From the next 100 most used words (from the Dolch list)

after	long
am	may
away	Mr
because	once
black	play
bring	read
don't	round
far	saw
fell	should
fly	soon
gave	tell
going	thing
green	time
head	under
house	walk
keep	wish
left	work

**At this level,
adults can**

read and understand
short, straightforward texts on
familiar topics

read and obtain information
from short documents, familiar
sources and signs and symbols

in texts such as public signs and
notices, lists, forms, notes,
records, e-mails, simple
narratives, letters and diagrams

An example of an integrated activity for reading   E2

Teaching focus

Text: characteristics of instructional texts: layout devices, use of graphics along with print

Sentence: the staged structure of instructions; *do*s and *don't*s; short sentences for directness

Word: how meaning is built up by words associated with the subject; how context can be used to help deduce meaning of individual words; sound–letter correspondence: long vowels, consonant blends; how word structure can be used to work out meaning: compound words, prefixes and suffixes

The text can be used as one of several on different topics to exemplify instructions encountered in work, home and social contexts.

- Ask learners in pairs to look at their copy of the text for 20 seconds, concentrating on the graphic images, then turn the text over and share initial thoughts with their partner on the subject matter and type of text. Pool impressions as a group including the use of the flame images and consider where such a text might be found, e.g. in a leaflet or poster from the fire service, on a label for a new chip pan.

- One way of engaging learners with detailed reading of this sort of text is to take the visual shape as a starting point (maybe using a large-print version which all the group can see). Invite learners to discuss how the text is set out – as a square divided into four sections, along with the image and two short sentences on their own. Starting with the bottom left quarter as Section 1 and numbering clockwise, all four sections can be looked at closely in turn. The image of the pan catches the eye and links with the flames in Section 2.

- Ask the group what they notice about the text inside the flames, e.g. largest print in the text, all in upper case, has three dots at the end. Read that section of text with the group, drawing attention to the *ch* sounds and the *–es* ending as necessary. Discuss why the section begins with *If-*, whether it forms a complete sentence and what the purpose of the three dots might be.

- Ask learners in pairs to try reading Section 3 and then look at it in detail, annotating their own texts to identify anything they find interesting about the layout, the sentences or the individual words. Share what people have noticed, drawing attention as necessary to: the way this section links with the previous one, telling the reader what to do and what not to do if their chip pan catches fire; the use of different font sizes; how you identify a negative instruction; the use of bullets to emphasise the list of 'to do' points; the significance of their order and the use of a complete sentence for each; the silent letter in *wring*; how the figures *30*, along with the context, might help the reader to work out the word *minutes*. (Although imperative verbs and second person are not explicit in the standards until Entry 3, learners might notice the repeated pattern of words that tell the reader what to do; in which case the teacher might decide to introduce the concept of imperative verbs at this stage.)

- Ask the learners to read the fourth section, and in a pair underline all the words that indicate that these are negative instructions. Discuss as a group, drawing attention as necessary to such points as: the use of four short sentences again; the relationship between *Do Not* in Section 3 and the shortened form *Don't* in Section 4, and why the writer might have chosen to use the different forms; the use of the word *never*; the longer words

IF YOUR CHIP PAN CATCHES FIRE...

DO NOT MOVE PAN OR USE WATER
- Turn off heat.
- Wring out a wet cloth.
- Place over pan.
- Leave it to cool for 30 minutes.

REMEMBER
- Never fill a pan more than a third full of fat or oil.
- Don't let it overheat.
- Don't leave it unattended.
- Never use wet chips.

Fire kills. Think about it

Reproduced by kind permission of the Home Office

(*re+member*, *over+heat* and *un+attend+ed*), and how looking at their structure can help to de-code them; sound–letter correspondence in *pan* and *fat,* in the long vowel sounds in *leave* and *heat*, and *oil,* the repeated sound and spelling in *or* and *more.* (Further work to reinforce understanding of word structure and sound–letter correspondence can be covered via games and exercises, as a group activity, or for individual self-study as necessary.)

- Read the whole text with the group again and ask learners to pick out all the words associated with heat, cold, wet, food and cooking, pointing out how these words build up the sense and context of the text. Demonstrate how learners' prior knowledge of cooking, heat, fat can all be applied to help them decode unknown words and make sense of the text.

- Ask everyone to re-read the whole text to themselves to try to memorise the instructions. Then, in pairs, one person turns their text over and explains from memory to the other what you mustn't do if you want to avoid your chip pan catching fire in the first place. The other person then explains what to do and not to do if your chip pan does catch fire.

- The text can also be used in comparison with other instructional texts, to evaluate which the group find most effective, and why.

Links with speaking, listening and discussion

Examining the text provides opportunity for learners to listen and speak with each other in straightforward exchanges, to follow and listen for detail in short explanations by the teacher and to ask questions to clarify understanding if necessary.

As they become familiar with the features of instructional texts through their reading, they can compare these with spoken instructions, noting how both are organised in sequence and both use verbs to 'tell' people what to do. Comparing the processes of following written and spoken instructions can also make learners more conscious of the difference between the contexts, such as being able to refer back to a written text but having to remember when listening, and knowing how to ask for clarification if needed.

Links with writing

Learners come to recognise and understand the features of written instructions through reading and can use this knowledge to begin to compose their own instructional texts. In turn, this provides an opportunity to compare the processes of writing down instructions and giving them orally.

At this level, adults can

read and understand
short, straightforward texts on familiar topics accurately and independently

read and obtain information
from everyday sources

in texts such as forms, notes, records, e-mails, narratives, letters, diagrams, simple instructions, short reports

| Text Focus | **Reading comprehension** | **Rt/E3** |

Skills, knowledge and understanding

Adults should be taught to:

❶ trace and understand the main events of chronological, continuous descriptive and explanatory texts of more than one paragraph

 – understand that meaning is built up through a text

 – understand the significance of the openings and endings of texts to overall meaning

 – understand that own knowledge (personal, contextual, phonological, grammatical, graphical) can be used to work out, predict and check the meaning of texts

❷ recognise the different purposes of texts at this level

 – understand that different texts have different purposes, e.g. to inform, explain, instruct, entertain, describe, persuade

 – understand that texts of the same form can have different purposes, e.g. a letter

❸ recognise and understand the organ-isational features and typical language of instructional texts, e.g. use of imperatives and second person

 – understand the different ways of presenting instructions, e.g. lists, numbered points, bullets, diagrams with arrows

 – know that the content of instructional texts may be laid out in different ways, not always left to right across the whole page

❹ identify the main points and ideas, and predict words from context

 – understand that some parts of texts may be more important to overall meaning than others

 – understand that the first sentence of a paragraph often introduces a new point/idea

 – understand that context and their own knowledge can help predict unfamiliar words

❺ understand and use organisational features to locate information (e.g. contents, index, menus)

 – understand that organisational features occur in different places within a text

 – understand the purpose of different organisational features and know that they work at different levels of detail, e.g. content, index, headings

Example

Read and understand the main events in a continuous text encountered in their own life, e.g. a school news-sheet for parents, a charity leaflet, a letter.

Select appropriate texts to suit their own purposes in daily life, e.g. newspaper, telephone directory, computer manual, tourist information leaflet.

Use instructional texts to complete tasks in their own life, e.g. recipes, rules, instructions for the use of equipment or products, route finder, directions.

Get the gist of a text and know what to do with it, e.g. health and safety notice at work, flier advertising a 'special offer', hospital/dental appointment letter.

Find a place on a street map by looking up the name in the index to locate the page and map reference.

Select an appropriate option from an on-screen menu (e.g. open link to other relevant information).

Sample activities

- Read a text of more than one paragraph with their teacher and other learners, discuss it and share responses (e.g. opening/extract from a story, newspaper report, section of holiday brochure).

- Read a narrative text and summarise the main events for their teacher and other learners.

- Read a selection of texts with the endings missing. Choose an ending for each from a range of alternatives. Read the completed texts and discuss reasons for the choice of ending with their teacher and other learners.

- Use a text-to-speech engine to check their understanding and reading of a text.

- Read a variety of short texts with different purposes. Decide when each might be relevant in their own life.

- In pairs, look at different sorts of letters delivered to home. Note their features and decide on any action/response, e.g. an official letter, circular letter, personal letter.

- Select their own preferred text and read it for pleasure or entertainment.

- In a pair or group, look at some different types of simple instructional texts on paper and/or screen. Compare layout, format, font, illustrations, and express a preference.

- Collect their own examples of instructional texts from home and work. Identify organisational features and relate these to the context of use. Discuss with their teacher/other learners.

- Put a sample of instructions to the test by following them, e.g. how to use a public telephone, vending/bank machines, load and play a video, etc.

- Use and insert bullet points (using icon and button) to separate and sequence a set of instructions.

- Read an appropriate text (e.g. a letter or simple article, an advert, a CD ROM or web page) and highlight the main points/ideas.

- Assemble a coherent text from cards, some containing the main point/idea/topic sentence and some with supporting detail.

- Read a simple continuous text and summarise the content for another person.

- Identify organisational features with teacher and other learners; discuss their function and locate examples in real texts.

- Select a topic of need/interest, e.g. when researching a topic for writing or discussion. Use the contents list and/or index in an information text to find relevant material, e.g. in a book on pet care, a simple history or science text, a travel guide.

- Practise locating and choosing items from a text, e.g. a meal from a take-away menu, an article on an order form, a regular feature in a magazine.

- Find an address (e.g. of an employer, of an organisation) from different sources such as a local trade directory, the Yellow Pages, a telephone directory, their own address book.

At this level, adults can

read and understand
short, straightforward texts on familiar topics accurately and independently

read and obtain information
from everyday sources

in texts such as forms, notes, records, e-mails, narratives, letters, diagrams, simple instructions, short reports

Text Focus	Reading comprehension	Rt/E3

Skills, knowledge and understanding

Adults should be taught to:

6 skim read title, headings and illustrations to decide if material is of interest

– understand that many texts are not meant to be read from end to end

– know that different features of a text provide clues to its contents and that illustrations contribute to meaning

7 scan texts to locate information

– understand that it is not always necessary to read every word

– know that headings, sub-headings and key words give clues about content

8 obtain specific information through detailed reading

– understand that it is sometimes necessary to read every word, or every word in a relevant section when located

9 relate an image to print and use it to obtain meaning

– understand that images are part of a text and provide meaning

Example

Select a holiday brochure from a range of other brochures.

Scan a cinema listing to find the title of a film.

Locate and read specific information, e.g. listings in a local newspaper.

Check details of the date and time of an appointment from a letter or card.

Use a picture in a TV guide to help locate the date and time of a programme.

Use symbols/diagrams/pictures on household products or equipment to help follow instructions on use.

Sample activities

- Skim pages in a newspaper to get an impression of the overall type of content from headings and pictures, e.g. news, sport, TV listings, letters, small ads.

- Skim a selection of texts for gist and overall impression, e.g. leaflet for tourist attraction, booklet on wild life, parish/community magazine. Discuss their general impression of content and purpose with their teacher or another learner.

- Identify current items in the news, then scan recent papers to locate articles on those items.

- Scan simple texts on paper or screen on a subject of interest/use and highlight relevant headings, key words and phrases that give clues to content. Use the same texts (or extracts of texts) to then read again word by word, using sentence- and word-level strategies to get at detailed meaning.

Reading techniques

As learners become more confident in their reading, they can learn to apply a range of techniques in order to extract from texts the information they need.

Learners need to understand that it is not necessary to read every word to obtain meaning from a text or to locate information. They need to practise the following techniques:

1. *Skimming* – reading quickly in order to find out what the text is about. Skimming can also take in features such as headings, subheadings and illustrations to obtain an overview of the subject matter.

2. *Scanning* – to locate specific information, making use of key words.

3. *Detailed reading* – reading carefully to aid understanding. When reading for information, detailed reading usually follows scanning. Some texts, such as instructions, need to be read in detail throughout.

- Read items of interest on Teletext. Practise reading pages with multiple screens, using the HOLD button if necessary.

- Share their own experiences of needing to read for detail (e.g. an important letter, a legal agreement). In pairs, read a business letter, e.g. from a utility company announcing reduced prices and changes to payment methods. Decide which information should be remembered and highlight it. Discuss with the group.

- Identify and locate individual specific critical information, e.g. the time of the last bus, the due date of a payment, the location of an event.

- Using images and text extracts, match related pairs and discuss how image adds to meaning, e.g. engine diagram to car manual, icons to menu bars, photograph to article, zodiac sign to horoscope, view of a place to description.

- Find information from illustrated texts, e.g. from weather forecasts in newspaper or on screen. For example, *Stacey is a tour guide in New York. Will she need an umbrella tomorrow? Nicolai is a farmer near Kiev. Will his crops stay dry this week?*

- Use a map to find information, e.g. the location of a specific shop in a shopping centre.

- Use the photos and other images on an opening web page to find a section of interest, e.g. sport, weather, money. Record/cache the image and the section.

read and understand
short, straightforward texts on
familiar topics accurately and
independently

read and obtain information
from everyday sources

in texts such as forms, notes,
records, e-mails, narratives,
letters, diagrams, simple
instructions, short reports

| Sentence Focus | **Grammar and punctuation** | **Rs/E3** |

Skills, knowledge and understanding

Adults should be taught to:

**❶ recognise and understand the
organisational features and typical
language of instructional texts (e.g.
use of imperatives, second person)**

- understand that instructional texts have
  particular language features, and be able to
  recognise them

- understand that their own knowledge of
  these features can be applied to help gain
  meaning from other instructional texts

- know and use the term *verb* and
  understand its importance as an essential
  feature of a sentence which conveys the
  action

- understand that verbs also convey time in a
  sentence: past, present, future

**❷ use implicit and explicit knowledge of
different types of word (e.g. linking words
[connectives], nouns, verbs, adjectives),
of word order, and of possible plausible
meanings, to help decode unfamiliar
words and predict meaning**

- understand that grammatical patterns,
  word order, types of word and meanings
  are inter-related and that only certain
  types of words and certain meanings will
  make sense in any particular place in a
  sentence

**❸ use punctuation and capitalisation to aid
understanding**

- understand that different punctuation marks
  are used for different purposes and know
  their names, including: *speech marks* to
  mark off what a speaker says from the
  surrounding text; *commas* to separate
  words in a list, or parts of a sentence

- understand that punctuation relates to
  sentence structure and text type to help the
  reader make sense of the written text, and
  apply this understanding in their own
  reading

Example

Recognise the language of instructions in
their own life, e.g.:

- *Write in block capitals.*

- *Put the CD in the drive.*

- *Empty contents into a saucepan and stir
  gently over a low heat.*

Read a simple continuous text written in
sentences (e.g. a newspaper article) and
get most of the sense even if they are not
able to read every word.

Recognise when questions are being asked
on a form by noting the question mark and
using this information to help their reading
and predict meaning, e.g. *How long have you
lived at your present address?*

Sample activities

- Read some simple instructions closely. Highlight examples of key sentence and language features, e.g.: opening statement of purpose; individual sentences often convey separate steps; the reader is addressed directly (in the second person); the reader is told what to do (imperative verbs).

- Practise recognising commands by sorting phrases and sentences into two separate lists of commands and statements using a computer, e.g. *Check the form, Take care, We'll meet you at 4pm, Complete in BLOCK CAPITALS, Sorry I missed you*, etc.

- Complete a cloze exercise in which all missing words are verbs, some in the imperative, some in simple present and past tenses. Read to check for sense.

- Read a short text in which certain words have been masked out. Keep going, then go back and guess the words using the context and their knowledge of word order and sentence patterns. Discuss the choice of words with the teacher/other learners.

- Practise how to monitor their own reading for sense and self-correction, becoming used to 'listening' internally to their own reading to spot errors of sense.

- Read some text extracts from everyday experience in which potentially tricky words have been highlighted. Read in pairs and apply knowledge of context, illustrations, grammatical understanding to work out any unknown words. Discuss the process, e.g.:

[From instructions for a vacuum cleaner]

. . . For cleaning awkward *places remove handle and insert tool adapter into end of hose. Attach tools as required.*

Awkward must relate to *places* and so is likely to be an adjective giving some information about *places*. Knowledge of context plus diagrams might suggest *'hard to reach'* places, which in turn might suggest *awkward*, a phonetically irregular word.

- Choose a text. Highlight the words that are difficult. Cut and paste them out of the text. Read the text again with the blank spaces, and record how much you understand.

- Read a range of different simple texts (e.g. a form, a letter, an extract from a story/article, a poem); highlight the punctuation. Discuss this with their teacher/other learners and identify some 'rules' about punctuation that can be written up as reference list.

- Underline/highlight direct speech on paper or screen, in different types of text, and consider its effect, e.g. in a fanzine or simplified magazine article about a celebrity, in a promotional text (e.g. *Mr C of Bradford said, "............................."*)

read and understand
short, straightforward texts on familiar topics accurately and independently

read and obtain information
from everyday sources

in texts such as forms, notes, records, e-mails, narratives, letters, diagrams, simple instructions, short reports.

| Word Focus | Vocabulary, word recognition and phonics | Rw/E3 |

Skills, knowledge and understanding

Adults should be taught to:

Example

❶ recognise and understand relevant specialist key words

– understand that some words are more important than others in particular contexts

– know what key specialist words are relevant, e.g. at work, specific to a job, health

– understand that knowledge of word origins, shared roots, word structure (e.g. prefixes, suffixes) can help with reading some key specialist words

Read and understand key words at work, e.g. health and safety.

❷ read and understand words and phrases commonly used on forms

– know that some words and phrases are commonly used on forms

Read and understand words and phrases commonly used on forms, e.g. *occupation, employer, make payable to, direct debit, block capitals.*

❸ use a dictionary to find the meaning of unfamiliar words

– understand alphabetical order

– understand the importance of the alphabetical order of letters within a word

Find the meaning of unknown words in their personal reading.

❹ use first- and second-place letters to find and sequence words in alphabetical order

– understand alphabetical order

– understand the importance of the alphabetical order of letters within a word

Find a service in the Yellow pages, e.g. plumber, printer.

Find words in a dictionary.

❺ use a variety of reading strategies to help decode an increasing range of unfamiliar words

– understand that effective readers draw on several sources of knowledge to help them make sense of unfamiliar words besides looking at the individual words themselves: clues from context, experience, text and sentence structure

– apply knowledge of sound and letter patterns and of structure of words, including compounds, root words, grammatical endings, prefixes, suffixes, syllable divisions to help decode words

Read common words with silent letters, e.g. *gnash, knife, knee, debt, receipt, write, wrist*

Read words with common prefixes, e.g. *un-, dis-, mis-,* and suffixes, e.g. *-ness, -less, -ly, -ful.*

Read and relate words with the same root, e. g. *hope/hopeful/hopeless/hopefully.*

Read common compound words such as *underneath, airport, whiteboard.*

Read an advertisement for a service in a directory, be able to decode some unfamiliar words and decide which company to choose (e.g. for car accident insurance repairs).

Sample activities

- Identify and read their own list of key specialist words.
- Match words from their own list with definitions and the context of use, e.g. safety helmet, customer service point.
- Identify any words from own key specialist words which have shared roots, and discuss structure and origin, e.g. *danger, dangerous; electricity, electric, electrician; produce, producer, product, production.*

- Match cards with a word or phrase commonly used on forms to a set of cards containing definitions.
- Match words and abbreviations to their meaning, e.g. *PTO, NI No., Overleaf.*
- Read and complete a form.

- From their own reading make a list of unknown words. Look up the meanings in a dictionary and make their own reference list of words and definitions. Write a sentence using each word correctly.
- Match words to definitions, using a dictionary to check on meanings, if necessary.
- Make use of the Thesaurus in Microsoft Word to check the meaning of words in a selected text.

- Sort a list of words with the same initial letter into alphabetical order.
- Sort a list of words on the computer into alphabetical order.
- Put their own key specialist words into alphabetical order.
- Find words starting with the same initial letter in a dictionary.
- Sort a list of names of people who have sent you e-mails. Then use the automatic sort function to check your answers.

- Add prefixes to a list of words to create new ones and explain their meaning.
- Raise awareness of word structure by:
  - matching words with common prefixes to a word that means the opposite, e.g. *appear/ disappear, tidy/untidy;*
  - underlining words with suffixes in their own reading;
  - identifying groups of words with shared roots; underlining root words in words with prefixes and suffixes;
  - splitting compound words into two to discuss their likely origins; joining words to make known compound words and experimenting with coining some useful new ones.
- In pairs, read some short texts from daily life (e.g. Yellow Pages entry, advertising flier, extract from a letter or story, some appliance instructions), photocopied on to A3 paper. Read a text once for general sense, circling any unfamiliar words. Read again and draw a line from each circled word out to the margin; copy out the word in large print in the margin. Discuss everything that can be worked out about the word, annotating it to demonstrate points, e.g. underline any familiar bits, divide into root and suffix/prefix or compound parts, underline a plural or verb ending. Reread the word in the context of its sentence or position. Decide on the most likely reading, using a dictionary to help as necessary. Reread whole text for sense. Discuss decisions with teacher.

read and understand
short, straightforward texts on familiar topics accurately and independently

read and obtain information from everyday sources

in texts such as forms, notes, records, e-mails, narratives, letters, diagrams, simple instructions, short reports.

An example of an integrated activity for reading E3

Teaching focus

Text: the structure of chronological texts, use of paragraphs and how meaning is built up in a narrative; the use of pictures to illustrate events and characters in a story

Sentence: variety of sentence structure to maintain interest; how certain punctuation signals a character is speaking in a story; the use of adjectives for description

Word: how to use word structure and knowledge of related words to help get at meaning; use of dictionary for unfamiliar words

This text is an extract from a complete short narrative that might be used with a group or individual to practise reading for enjoyment, following a story to its conclusion and discussing it.

In the mirror his face was a mass
of cuts and bruises.
He looked as if he had been in an accident.
While Nell stared at him,
blood began to drip from his wounds.
'What's up, little Nell?' he asked.
'You look as if you've seen a ghost.
Aren't you going to give me a good night kiss?'
His breath smelled of whisky.
Face to face he looked just as he always did.
A bit fleshy, a little red around the nose.
There was no sign of any blood.

Anna came to join them, doing up her coat.
She was over forty,
but still a beautiful woman.
Nell froze. In the mirror
Anna too was horrible to look at.

Great pieces of glass stuck out from her cheeks.
One eye was closed, and the other. . .

Nell ran from the hall,
leaving Tom to say goodbye

From *Mirror, Mirror* by Iris Howden
(Hodder & Stoughton, 1996). Reproduced by kind permission of the publisher.

- Recap with the learners what has happened so far, who the characters are and what their relationships are to each other, identifying anything that remains unclear up to this point.
- Ask the learners to try reading the two paragraphs for themselves, using knowledge of what has happened so far and the picture to help follow the story, noting down any unfamiliar words in their personal dictionaries for later reference. Discuss together impressions of this extract: who is involved, and what is happening.
- Read both paragraphs aloud to the learners asking them to listen for names of the characters, to be ready to summarise the episode and to consider how this part ends. Discuss the story line in more detail. Who is 'he'? Whose shoes are we standing in when we read the story? Ask them to identify any questions in their minds.

- Follow the text in closer detail together, in order to model the reading process for learners, e.g.: *What does the first sentence tell you? What does the second sentence add?* Look closely at *bruises* and *accident* as necessary, noting the *–ui–* pattern and the double *–cc–*, the first *–c–* sounded as [k], the second as [s]. (Self-study exercises can be set as necessary to reinforce pronunciation of similar sounding *–ui–* words, and dictionary work to investigate other *–acc–* words with a similar pronunciation, e.g. *access, accent, accept, accelerate.*)

- Give learners some Post-it strips and ask them to place these under the bits of text that represent direct speech, reminding them of how speech marks are used to mark off the words a character says from the rest of the story. In pairs, ask them to read these to each other using a voice that represents how they think the character might say them, bearing in mind the question mark and the information given in the sentence immediately after the direct speech.

- Ask readers to read to the end of Paragraph 1. If they had to paint a picture of the man as he appeared in the mirror and then of what he looked like when Nell saw him face to face, what details would they include in each? Which particular words convey these details?

- Ask learners to read the whole of Paragraph 2 and to be ready to answer these questions: *Why does a new paragraph start here? How is Anna different in the mirror from what she is face to face? How does Nell react when she sees Anna in the mirror? Why is one sentence incomplete? Why is one sentence shorter than the others?* Then discuss the answers together, checking that people have understood properly and identifying any difficult words. Draw attention to the adjectives *beautiful* and *horrible* and ask learners to identify related words (e.g. *beauty, horror, horrifying*) and discuss the forms and meanings. (Games and investigations can be used to reinforce understanding of word roots and suffixes and how different types of words (nouns, adjectives, adverbs, verbs) are sometimes related etymologically and share common elements.)

Finish the discussion by asking learners to predict what will happen next (and remind them of the predictions before reading the next episode). Ask them to write definitions for any new words added to their personal dictionaries. They could be asked to read a further section of the story for the next class and to come along ready to summarise what happens and to raise any points or questions.

Links to speaking, listening and discussion

The activities round the text involve speaking, listening and discussion at each stage, providing opportunity for learners to listen for both gist and detail in narratives, to listen and respond to points of view and to make relevant contributions to group discussion. Specific spoken communication activities could also be planned that relate to reading narrative and would extend learners' experience of following a story line and talking about it, e.g.: invite an outside speaker to tell a story or relate an experience and discuss it with the group; listen to and discuss a tape-recorded story; ask learners to recount an experience either in pairs or to the group.

Links with writing

As they become more familiar with texts that have a narrative structure (e.g. story, biography, autobiography), learners can plan and draft their own narrative texts, fictional or experiential, providing opportunity to sequence chronological writing organised in paragraphs, and to maintain tense consistency and subject–verb agreement. Composing and editing on screen to produce a text (e.g. to go in a Christmas/end-of-year anthology) would provide a real context in which to emphasise the importance of planning, editing and proof-reading.

The Adult Literacy
Core Curriculum

See also in the key skills: Communication key skills level 1
Part A: In reading and obtaining information...
Part B: C1.2

LEVEL 1 *At this level, adults can*

read and understand
straightforward texts of varying
length on a variety of topics
accurately and independently

read and obtain information
from different sources

in reports, instructional,
explanatory and persuasive texts

 Text Focus **Reading comprehension**   **Rt/L1**

Skills, knowledge and understanding

Adults should be taught to:

**1 trace and understand the main
events of continuous descriptive,
explanatory and persuasive texts**

– understand that meaning is developed
through a text, and it is necessary to
sustain concentration and relate the parts
of a text to each other in order to trace the
main events and get an overall sense of
what the text is about

– understand that personal knowledge and
experience, knowledge of context, grammar
and vocabulary all contribute to
determining overall sense

– understand that meaning in texts can be
implied as well as explicitly stated

**2 recognise how language and other
textual features are used to achieve
different purposes (e.g. to instruct,
explain, describe, persuade)**

– understand that choice of language and
textual features reflect the purpose of a text

– know that different types of text use
different sorts of language, structural and
presentational devices

– understand that readers can choose
different sorts of texts to read for pleasure,
depending on their tastes and interests,
e.g., imaginative texts: stories, novels,
poems; factual texts: biographies, travel
writing, information texts

**3 identify the main points and specific
detail, and infer meaning from images
which is not explicit in the text**

– understand that some texts are structured
around main points that are expanded or
illustrated by specific detail

– understand that in some texts and
situations only the main points are
essential to get the meaning, whereas in
others every detail requires careful reading

– understand that images can be used to
convey additional information to that in the
printed text

Example

Read and understand a written description
in their own daily life and come to a
conclusion based on its contents,
e.g. choose a holiday after reading a
brochure.

Be able to distinguish between an objective
description and a persuasive description,
e.g. a description of what is an NVQ
portfolio, compared with a description in an
advert.

Read a report from an appraisal or job
review and distinguish the main points from
examples/details.

Sample activities

- Read a continuous text of at least three paragraphs, e.g. a section from an information text on a topic of interest. Summarise the overall content to the teacher/other learners and give an opinion on it.

- In pairs, each read the same selection of texts (e.g. an announcement from a council news-sheet, a magazine feature on child-care, a travel account). Summarise the main event/points, then identify which parts required 'reading between the lines'.

- In pairs, annotate enlarged photocopies of different types of text (e.g. a job vacancy, an estate agent's description, rules for a sport, a poem), by circling/highlighting/making notes on particular features of language, structure, format and layout. Discuss their findings with their partner.

- Experiment with reading a range of texts for pleasure. Keep a reading record (on paper or screen) of titles and authors of texts read, and a brief note of their 'enjoyment rating'. Use the list for reference for choosing future texts.

- Open a set of documents in a folder and list whether they are letters, memos, e-mails, notes or legal documents.

- Read an explanation of a process. Highlight the main points and use them to explain the process to someone else.

- Read a selection of texts and decide where it is enough to understand the main points and where all details are important (e.g. a review of a film, instructions on how to give the kiss of life).

- Read and discuss in pairs some texts that include images (e.g. diagrams in instructions, cartoon illustrations in Inland Revenue leaflet, photographs in a feature on home decoration/ improvement) and decide what the images add to the print text and how essential they are to the overall purpose and meaning.

- Use Clip Art or another image file to choose and insert images to a range of texts.

The Adult Literacy
Core Curriculum

See also in the key skills: Communication key skills level 1
Part A: In reading and obtaining information . . .
Part B: C1.2

LEVEL 1   *At this level, adults can*

read and understand
straightforward texts of varying length on a variety of topics accurately and independently

read and obtain information
from different sources

in reports, instructional, explanatory and persuasive texts

 Text Focus   **Reading comprehension**   **Rt/L1**

Skills, knowledge and understanding

Adults should be taught to:

4 use organisational and structural features to locate information (e.g. contents, index, menus, subheadings, paragraphs)

– understand that different kinds of text have different structural and organisational features, e.g. contents, index, menus, chapters, sections, 'pages'/layers in hypertext

– understand that different kinds of text require different methods of navigation, e.g. encyclopaedia in book form, links in hypertext

5 use different reading strategies to find and obtain information

– understand that there are different ways of reading for different purposes

– understand that skimming is for getting general gist and overall impression; scanning is for locating information

– understand that specific information is obtained through detailed reading

Example

Find weather forecast in a newspaper, on teletext, on a web site.

Find out specific information from a timetable.

Sentence Focus   **Grammar and punctuation**   **Rs/L1**

Skills, knowledge and understanding

Adults should be taught to:

1 use implicit and explicit grammatical knowledge (e.g. of different sentence forms, types of word, verb tense, word order) along with own knowledge and experience to predict meaning, try out plausible meanings, and to read and check for sense

– understand that knowledge of sentence patterns and word order can help to predict unknown words and get meaning from text

– understand that some sentence structures and types of word will occur more often in some types of text than others

– understand that grammatical and semantic clues can be used alongside whole-text and word-level clues to make sense of individual words and of complete sentences

– understand the terms *tense, negative, adverb, pronoun, phrase*

Example

Read with understanding a variety of straightforward continuous texts encountered in their own life, e.g. a letter from their child's school, an insurance policy renewal.

Sample activities

- Identify some relevant individual information and use a local directory to find it, e.g. hairdresser, plumber, local council.

- In pairs, look for the same information (e.g. on train times, course programmes, football results) from different sources (e.g. timetables, teletext, web page, prospectus, newspaper). Compare and evaluate the various processes and the quality/usefulness of the information.

- Find and locate specific information to use in their own writing from a CD-ROM or college intranet.

- Undertake guided 'web hunts' designed to practise finding information on the web.

- In pairs, undertake a timed exercise in skimming. Each skim as many of a selection of short texts as they can get through in the time. Make brief note of the subject matter; discuss their results.

- In pairs, set each other a task to locate some information from print text and/or screen, on a topic of interest to the task setter (e.g. how to grow a particular plant, the origins of test cricket). Present the information to the partner (by marking print text with 'post-its' or making notes/printing key pages from screen). The partner judges how useful/relevant/interesting the information is and identifies any gaps.

- Use real contexts or case studies to identify specific information needed. Locate and read it (using sentence- and word-level reading strategies as necessary) in order to, e.g. choose a holiday, plan a journey, write a letter, make a hospital visit, phone the council to ask them to remove some rubbish.

Sample activities

- Highlight imperatives, adverbs and adverbial phrases in an instructional text and discuss their effect, e.g. *lift carefully; place the side panel at right angles to the front; lightly whisk for five minutes.*

- Investigate the use of negative verbs, e.g. in warning notices, small print conditions on insurance policies, and discuss their purpose.

- Highlight verbs and identify tense in a narrative and a descriptive text. Compare findings with their teacher/other learners.

- Annotate a persuasive text to indicate how the order of points is developed, by highlighting linking words and phrases, e.g. *therefore, however, if, unless, because, finally, whatever, as a result of.*

- Compare sentence length and structures in a story written for a very young child with one for an older child. Discuss their findings and draw some conclusions.

- When reading different types of text underline unknown/difficult words and phrases and discuss with partner how to use surrounding sentence, context, text- and word-level clues to interpret these, using a dictionary to check meanings where necessary, e.g.: [from an invitation to an Open Afternoon at a local school]

  At 2.30pm the Mayor, Councillor Mrs Jane Brown, will be at the school to see the sculpture that has been made this term by our Artist in <u>Residence</u>, Mr Wayne Stockwell, working with the children.

  We would like you to walk round the school to see the <u>splendidly refurbished</u> Literacy and Numeracy areas, which some of our parents have helped decorate, and look at displays of children's work.

See also in the key skills: Communication key skills level 1
Part A: In reading and obtaining information . . .
Part B: C1.2

LEVEL 1 *At this level, adults can*

read and understand
straightforward texts of varying length on a variety of topics accurately and independently

read and obtain information
from different sources

in reports, instructional, explanatory and persuasive texts

Sentence Focus Grammar and punctuation Rs/L1

Skills, knowledge and understanding

Adults should be taught to:

2 use punctuation to help their understanding

– understand the function of the omissive apostrophe to indicate a contracted word form in texts written in informal style

– know and use the term *apostrophe*

– secure knowledge of end-of-sentence punctuation and commas in helping to make sense of continuous text

Example

Note the use of the apostrophe for missing letters as a signal of an informal style, in texts encountered in daily life, e.g. notes from workmates or members of family, 'chatty' promotional letters, e-mails.

Word Focus Vocabulary Rw/L1

Skills, knowledge and understanding

Adults should be taught to:

1 use reference material to find the meaning of unfamiliar words

– know there are different sources of information for word meanings, e.g. dictionary, glossary, key

– understand the structure of standard dictionary entries, the abbreviations used, and the sort of information provided about each word

– understand the purpose of glossaries and where they are likely to be found

2 recognise and understand the vocabulary associated with different types of text, using appropriate strategies to work out meaning

– understand the types of word likely to be used in different kinds of text, depending on the context and purpose

– understand the use and effect of specialist vocabulary in particular text types

Example

Look up meaning of specialist words in a glossary, e.g. when reading an information text on an unfamiliar subject.

Read and understand specialist and explanatory vocabulary in a leaflet from the dentist on care of teeth.

3 recognise and understand an increasing range of vocabulary, applying knowledge of word structure, related words, word roots, derivations, borrowings

– understand that some words are related to each other in form and meaning and use this knowledge to help understand new words

– understand that prefixes can provide clues to meaning

– understand that languages borrow words from each other

Follow and understand a menu that includes borrowed words, e.g. pesto sauce, lamb kebab, chili tacos, spiced mango.

Sample activities

- Read some e-mails sent or received by themselves or others and highlight the apostrophes that indicate a letter (or letters) has (have) been omitted. Compare the number of contracted forms in the e-mails with the number in a formal letter, e.g. from a bank, building society.

- Read a selection of different types of straightforward texts; highlight end-of-sentence punctuation and commas. Compare the incidence and usage between texts and discuss with their teacher and other learners; make note of any new usage or 'rules' encountered.

Sample activities

- Read a text with some key terms omitted. Using a list of possible words, select suitable ones to complete the sense, using a dictionary to check meanings as necessary.

- Identify some unfamiliar technical and specialist words in an information text and look up their meanings in a glossary; record definitions for reference, e.g. in their own personal glossary. Use each word in their own sentences to reinforce meaning.

- Select some words of personal interest from their own reading; check the meanings, origin and usage in a dictionary.

- Use the 'What's This' and 'Help Index' to find the meaning of words connected with the use of the computer (e.g. bookmark, CD ROM, hyperlink).

- Highlight technical and specialist vocabulary in an explanatory text and check meanings as necessary.

- Read some short arguments, e.g. from a Greenpeace leaflet. Discuss and highlight features of its vocabulary, e.g. collective nouns: *wildlife, people, society;* abstract nouns: *environment, evidence, truth.*

- Collect some persuasive texts, e.g. adverts, junk mail, charity appeals, and highlight the words in them that are intended to persuade.

- Underline words in a descriptive text that indicate a particular mood (e.g. for suspense, words such as *deserted, fearful, mysterious, dread,* etc.) and discuss the connotations of these words for the reader.

- Compare the use of descriptive vocabulary in imaginative and factual texts, e.g. a poem on a landscape with a geographical description of landscape features.

- Read words with a common root and use knowledge of prefixes, suffixes and verb forms to work out their meaning, e.g. *insure, insurance; comfort, comfortable, comforting, comforted.*

- Explore prefixes that provide clues to meaning, e.g. *tri–: tricycle, triangle, triceps, tripod; tele–: television, telescope, telepathy.*

- Use an etymological dictionary to explore origins of own specialist key words and to identify any other less familiar, related words.

- Identify words from own reading with similar patterns (e.g. *chr–* openings, *–tion* endings) and discuss with teacher pronunciations, letter patterns, origins.

- Use a predictive text program to explore prefixes and their use.

read and understand
straightforward texts of varying
length on a variety of topics
accurately and independently

read and obtain information
from different sources

in reports, instructional,
explanatory and persuasive texts

An example of an integrated activity for reading   L1

Teaching focus

Text: how text structure, layout and choice of language are related to purpose; how to identify and locate specific information in a persuasive text

Sentence: use of present tense, characteristic sentence structure of a persuasive text, how commas can help the reader make sense of a text

Word: vocabulary associated with promotional travel texts: descriptive words and phrases, over-worked phrases

This text could be used as one of several different persuasive texts, to build up learners' experience of promotional writing, how it works and what a reader might get from it.

- Assemble and copy the extracts on to A3 sheets for each learner and ask them in pairs to spend five minutes looking at the text overall, annotating it briefly to say what they think the main purpose is and the purpose of each section. Share observations as a group, looking at what information can be gleaned from scanning the picture and its text, the contents, titles, logos, before reading in more detail.

- Display the word *Mediterranean*, ask if anyone knows its meaning and explain its Latin origin; examine its structure and spelling. Have a map to hand to show where it is and which countries surround it. Invite learners to mention if they have ever visited any places in the region. Look at the name INSPOS (it is an invented place) and consider how you might work out it is a place name, but not an English one. Examine the structure, spelling and meaning of *incorporating, Self-catering, All-inclusive,* drawing attention to roots, prefixes and suffixes, use of hyphens, and where learners might have met these terms before.

- On the basis of this first examination, ask learners to speculate on which people would be likely to want to read this text in more detail. Display learners' initial thoughts for later reference (e.g. people who like the sun, people looking for a holiday in this part of the world, people who like swimming, etc.).

- Read out the section headed INSPOS to the group, asking them to listen particularly for factual information about the place. Pool facts and display them (e.g. on the coast, old harbour, wine-producing region, tavernas, bars, restaurants, less than an hour from the second largest town in the region, mountain caves). Invite the group to discuss as appropriate whether any of the suggestions are not exactly straight facts (e.g. *glorious* beach).

- Before asking learners to read the passage for themselves, display some of the longer or less familiar words (e.g. *unique, cosmopolitan, peninsula, crystalline, paradise, excursion, tranquility, souvenir, fascinating*). Look at the pronunciation, form and spelling of each one in turn, reading out the sentence where it occurs and asking people to suggest meanings from their own knowledge or from the context. Formulate a definition of each which learners can add to their personal dictionaries; draw attention to any particular applications of the words in this context (e.g. *Is **unique** really **unique** here? This **paradise** is not the original* **Paradise**).

- Ask the learners to now read the whole of this section in pairs, stopping at the end of each paragraph to discuss with their partner what they have read. Ask them to look particularly closely at the first sentence of each paragraph and make a note of such things as sentence type, length, use of commas, the way the sentence begins, verb tense. As well, highlight on their text any details they find interesting or appealing about the place, and check any other unfamiliar words in the dictionary.

CONTENTS

SAN INSPOS HOTEL

Amenities: The hotel is situated in a quiet area near the harbour and 1km from the beach, which is suitable for families with its golden sand and shallow waters. The hotel is close to restaurants and bars which makes it ideal for those searching for a relaxing daytime with everything close at hand for the late night reveller. See key for hotel facilities.

INSPOS

Want to get away from it all? Welcome to Inspos, our holiday jewel. Its old harbour has a unique, cosmopolitan atmosphere which draws visitors and locals alike to its many bars and restaurants. For those passionate about seafood, this is the perfect place to be. Fish is freshly caught and served in many of the local tavernas along with the opportunity to sample the local wines.

The peninsula of Inspos pierces the shimmering waters of the Mediterranean Sea. The jewel in the crown is the glorious beach which runs along the dramatic coastline for over 40km. Scented pines and wild flowers reach down to the golden sands whch are lapped by crystalline waters. This is a natural paradise, unspoilt and rarely crowded – a holiday maker's dream.

Less than an hour's drive away is Charma, the second largest town in the region, steeped in ancient history but also boasting a thriving modern shopping centre. The local Thursday market in the old town square is a must for all the family, especially for that really special souvenir. The Caves of Inspos are an unmissable excursion, high in the mountains above the coast.

Whether you're basking on the sun-drenched beaches or venturing inland for some fascinating sightseeing, Inspos promises to remain in your memory as a very special haven of tranquility.

(continued over page)

read and understand
straightforward texts of varying
length on a variety of topics
accurately and independently

read and obtain information
from different sources

in reports, instructional,
explanatory and persuasive texts

An example of an integrated activity for reading *(continued)*   **L1**

- Then discuss each paragraph with the group, looking at features of the opening sentences (e.g. the abbreviated question in Paragraph 1; the image in Paragraph 2; the order of the information in Paragraph 3; the opening, and length, of Paragraph 4, and the occurrence in it of *you're (you are)* and *your (belongs to you)*; the use of present tense in all), relating features to purpose and effect. Share the details learners have picked out and the impressions they have formed of the place. Discuss how convincing they find the information, and whether there are any phrases they have met before (e.g. *golden sands, perfect place, thriving modern shopping centre, sun-drenched beaches, haven of tranquility*).

- Ask learners to scan the information about the San Inspos Hotel, looking to see if it tells them where exactly it is and anything about its facilities, and whether on the strength of this they would choose to stay in it.

- Having read each part of the text, consider what further information a reader would be likely to need before deciding whether this is the holiday for them (e.g. prices, highest temperatures, nearest airport). Finish by going back to the group's earlier thoughts on who might be interested in this text. In the light of what learners have found out from their reading, discuss which age groups, interest groups, types of holiday maker might choose Inspos.

Links with speaking, listening and discussion

Activities involve listening to identify information and to understand explanations, responding to questions and making relevant contributions. This text would also provide opportunity for holding a discussion that goes beyond the text itself, e.g. on learners' ideal 'dream holiday', on the appeal of different parts of the world for different people. In turn, learners could be given a book list of literary travel writing for their own reading for pleasure, or a research task to find out about a place of particular interest to them, sharing what they find out with the group.

Links with writing

Having studied the features of a variety of persuasive texts, learners could be asked to prepare their own, on screen or paper, identifying a context for persuasion and a text type (e.g.: a letter from a charity asking for funds; a leaflet for a tourist attraction such as a theme park, museum, sporting event; a flier advertising a household service; a holiday advert in a magazine). Prepare a suitable text and try it out on fellow learners for its credibility and persuasive qualities. This would involve using language, format and structure suitable for the purpose and audience and would also require accurate proof-reading and legible text.

See also in the key skills: Communication key skills level 2
Part A: In reading and summarising information . . .
Part B: C2.2

At this level,
adults can

read and understand
a range of texts of varying
complexity accurately and
independently

read and obtain information
of varying length and detail from
different sources

in a wide range of text types

| Text Focus | **Reading comprehension** | **Rt/L2** |

Skills, knowledge and understanding

Example

Adults should be taught to:

1 trace and understand the main events
of continuous descriptive, explanatory
and persuasive texts

– understand that continuous texts may be
structured round a main event(s), idea(s),
theme(s)

– understand that it is sometimes necessary to
infer meaning which is not explicitly stated,
in order to arrive at a correct overall
understanding

– understand that judgements can be made
about texts from an overall understanding of
their content, by reflecting on what has been
read

Read a report on an issue of local
importance, follow the main ideas and get a
sense of the overall meaning.

2 identify the purpose of a text and infer
meaning which is not explicit

– understand that different kinds of text have
different purposes, that texts can have more
than one purpose, and that the real purpose
of some texts can be different from the
explicitly stated purpose

– understand that format, structure, vocabulary
and style provide clues to the purpose of a text

– understand that the relevance of a text
depends on the reader's purpose as well as
the purpose of the text

Recognise when an article in a newspaper
or magazine is being ironic or satirical,
e.g. a review apparently praising a TV
programme or film, but actually being
critical of it.

3 identify the main points and specific
detail

– understand the difference between main
points and specific detail as they occur in
different types of text, e.g. a letter, a safety
report, a rail timetable

– understand the importance of knowing when
it is sufficient to grasp the main points and
when the details are also important

– understand that knowledge of the
organisation and layout of different texts can
help distinguish main points from detail
(e.g. headings, topic sentences)

Distinguish the main points and details in
texts related to their own work, home and
learning, e.g. get details of a rock star's UK
tour from a web site; select the main points
from their child's school report to follow up at
parents' evening; note the main points from
an article related to a subject of study/
interest.

4 read an argument and identify the
points of view

– understand the characteristic structures of
written argument

– understand that texts presenting an
argument are adopting a particular point of
view

– understand the difference between
objective fact and opinion/point of view

Read about and distinguish the pros and
cons of an issue and come to their own
conclusion.

Sample activities

- Read a continuous text of at least five paragraphs (e.g. a section from an information text on a topic of their own interest/the opening pages of a story). Track the main events/points using a highlighter or underlining. Reflect on the overall meaning. Summarise the main events/points to the teacher/other learners and give own opinion on the text.

- In pairs, read some persuasive texts (e.g. publisher's 'blurb' on a book jacket/cover; leaflet on a local attraction). Get a sense of overall content, recognise that the descriptions are intentionally favourable and decide if they are persuaded to read the book/visit the attraction or not.

- Read a continuous text. Use a text window to summarise the passage as you read it. Save the summary as a separate document.

- Skim a selection of different types of text and categorise them by purpose from their general impression, e.g. an anti-abortion leaflet, a company report, a short story.

- In pairs, read in detail various texts, e.g. letters, extracts from reports, specialist or general interest articles, information texts. From a list of statements of purpose, select which ones apply to which texts, and whether these purposes are explicit or implied (e.g. *Is this text aiming to: give personal opinions/objective facts/make the reader laugh/flatter the reader/justify a position/explain a process/apologise for a mistake/complain?*). Discuss decisions with their teacher.

- Read an article/extract written for the general public on a subject of current scientific interest (e.g. mapping the human genome). Identify and highlight the main points (e.g. in topic sentences) in one colour, and specific details in another. Decide which are the three most important points learnt from the article and explain them to another person.

- Read a newspaper report (e.g. of a natural disaster/accident/high-profile incident). Identify and highlight the facts. Decide which are the main points and which specific detail.

- Read a range of viewpoints on a contentious issue (e.g. the siting/design of a new football stadium, fox hunting). Highlight verifiable facts in one colour and opinions/expressions of feeling in another. Read again to identify particular features of sentence structure and vocabulary related to expressing facts, and opinions and feelings. Then, in a group, organise a discussion around the topic, using these viewpoints as a starting point. Make some preparatory notes, based on the texts and the group discussion, and use them to plan and draft a piece of writing, presenting own views on the subject, on paper or screen. Proof-read and revise the writing.

- In pairs, from a cut-up text re-assemble the sequence of an argument (e.g. in a speech, campaign leaflet, article by a pressure group) so that points follow logically. Read the completed text for sense; identify viewpoints. Discuss with their partner and share their own views on the subject.

- Search the world-wide web for differing points of view on a subject, e.g. the effects of alcohol on health, web sites of political parties. Cut and paste key points that demonstrate the main points of view into a Word document.

See also in the key skills: Communication key skills level 2
Part A: In reading and summarising information . . .
Part B: C2.2

LEVEL 2 *At this level, adults can*

read and understand
a range of texts of varying complexity accurately and independently

read and obtain information
of varying length and detail from different sources

in a wide range of text types

Text Focus   **Reading comprehension**   **Rt/L2**

Skills, knowledge and understanding

Adults should be taught to:

⑤ **read critically to evaluate information, and compare information, ideas and opinions from different sources**

– understand that selection and presentation of information is rarely completely objective

– understand that information on the same topic from different sources may have different, even contradictory emphases

– understand the concept of bias and that it can be the result of what is left out of a text as well as what is there

⑥ **use organisational features and systems to locate texts and information**

– understand that information can be organised and referenced in different ways and in different layers of detail

– understand that different systems are used to organise whole texts, e.g. library systems, filing system in an office, on a computer

⑦ **use different reading strategies to find and obtain information (e.g. skimming, scanning, detailed reading)**

– understand the importance of choosing the best reading strategy for the purpose in terms of time and efficiency

– know how to skim for gist, scan to locate information, read in detail to select and judge relevance of specific information

– understand the importance of selecting and noting key points for future reference

Example

Recognise how the same story is presented differently by different newspapers.

Locate required information in a library.

Choose texts to read for pleasure from a library/bookshop/on-line book shop/book club.

Apply appropriate reading strategies to find the information needed (e.g. for an essay, to research an expensive purchase).

- Identify the key ways in which two different newspapers deal with the same story (e.g. location in paper, layout, selection of information, use of illustrations, choice of vocabulary and sentence structure, conclusions reached); discuss findings with other learners and consider reasons for the differences.

- In a group, critically compare some information from several sources on a current contentious subject (e.g. genetic engineering, film censorship, transport policies, causes of AIDS). Compare and evaluate texts by highlighting different aspects in different colours: selection of factual information, expressions of opinion, evidence of bias; then consider their own conclusions on the subject.

- Discuss various ways in which information is organised in libraries, and how the user can access this (e.g. books, magazines, web sites). Visit a library, as a group, and practise using the systems to locate specific texts and sites.

- Identify ways in which different types of text signal to the reader where specific information is (e.g. contents, index, bibliography, document files, web-site links). Practise using these to locate specific information from different texts to use in own writing, for a presentation, discussion or general interest.

Thinking about what you read

Judging what you read is often considered a higher-order skill or level of understanding, but most adults are aware, for example, that the purpose of an advert is to sell them something. This experience can be built on to teach people to evaluate what they read as a matter of course:

- What is it for?
- Where is it coming from?
- Who is it aimed at?
- What can I infer that isn't explicitly stated?
- Do I believe it?

An understanding of the concept of person and the writer's voice can be developed alongside decoding and in relation to different text types:

- Do I know who the writer is?
- Does it matter?
- Is the writer the same person as the narrator?
- Is the writer a named individual or a representative of an organisation/body/authority?
- Is the writer assuming a 'voice' for the occasion?

In continuous texts, readers can try to distinguish:

- main points from supporting detail
- facts from opinions
- conflicting viewpoints
- evidence of simplification, generalisation, manipulation, bias.

By this level, effective adult readers are using all their reading skills in a multi-fronted approach: their knowledge of the world, of text types, of sentence structures, vocabulary, sounds, knowledge of language and specific content. They are making sense of what they read and reflecting on its validity, relevance, quality. They are using what they read to further their lives, and to extend their understanding of life.

- In pairs or groups, identify a real task for which information is needed. Plan the information search, in stages, deciding which reading strategies are likely to be most efficient at each stage. Work through the stages:

  (a) Use catalogue/search engine to locate relevant titles.

  (b) Skim several titles for general impression and choose up to three that look relevant.

  (c) Scan these to locate any useful sections; mark with stickies or bookmark on screen.

  (d) Starting with the section that seems most useful, read carefully and critically in close detail.

  (e) While reading, write brief notes of the most important points and record the source: title, chapter/section, web site, page number, etc.

  (f) When deciding a whole page is relevant after reading it, photocopy it/paste it into a word-processing file, to read again later.

  (g) Highlight key words and phrases from their notes/photocopied pages/word file and sort the main points under relevant headings for future use.

The Adult Literacy
Core Curriculum

See also in the key skills: Communication key skills level 2
Part A: In reading and summarising information ...
Part B: C2.2

LEVEL 2

At this level, adults can

read and understand
a range of texts of varying complexity accurately and independently

read and obtain information
of varying length and detail from different sources

in a wide range of text types

Text Focus **Reading comprehension** **Rt /L2**

Skills, knowledge and understanding

Adults should be taught to:

8 summarise information from longer documents

– understand that summarising must be preceded by locating and selecting information through skimming, scanning and detailed reading

– understand that selection involves distinguishing the main points and supporting detail in the document

– understand that what to select and how best to present it in summary form will also depend on knowing the purpose and audience for the summary

Example

Summarise the key points (e.g. from a newspaper article/official report on a subject relevant to their own life) in order to discuss the issue at a meeting (e.g. re proposal to close a local school/post office/sell open land for building).

Sentence Focus **Grammar and punctuation** **Rs/L2**

Skills, knowledge and understanding

Adults should be taught to:

1 use implicit and explicit grammatical knowledge, alongside own knowledge and experience of context, to help follow meaning and judge the purpose of different types of text

– understand that some grammatical forms and types of word signal the level of formality of a text, e.g. passive verbs, third person, abstract nouns

– understand that specific grammatical devices are used to persuade, e.g. deliberate ambiguity, rhetorical questions, repetition

Example

Read and understand a newspaper report on some research into the safety of mobile phones.

2 use punctuation to help interpret the meaning and purpose of texts

– understand that certain punctuation is used for particular purposes in some text types, e.g. colon, semicolon, hyphen, dash, brackets, in lists, leaflets, brochures

– understand the range and function of the various punctuation used in written English, and the way 'rules' and attitudes change over time

Recognise in their own reading that information in brackets is usually less important than the surrounding text.

Sample activities

- Practise the summarising process using real tasks/contexts (e.g. related to writing/presentation/discussion activities) or case studies to identify suitable documents:

    (a) Use headings/sub-headings, topic sentences in paragraphs to identify the most important parts of a document for their purpose.

    (b) Highlight/underline and make notes of the main points plus any supporting information judged necessary.

    (c) Group related points under the same heading using bullets/numbering if helpful and/or draw a diagram (e.g. flow chart, spider diagram) to represent the main points and connections between them.

    (d) Use notes and diagrams to present a verbal or written summary to others or to complete another task.

    (Summarising from longer documents brings together skills of reading and writing, e.g. close reading, selection, note-making, recasting. It can result in a written or spoken product).

Sample activities

- Compare two texts on related subjects but with different levels of formality. Highlight grammatical features that convey formality/informality, e.g. second-person/third-person pronouns; active/passive verbs; abstract/concrete nouns; sentence length and complexity.

- Highlight active and passive verbs in some short texts; experiment with transforming them into each other. Discuss the effects and consider how the passive can conceal the agent of a sentence, e.g. *Ms X was repeatedly harassed and insulted.*

- Identify rhetorical questions in a newspaper article; turn them into statements and discuss the effect.

- Read a selection of promotional leaflets; annotate and classify the different sorts of punctuation marks used and decide if and how they contribute to the text's persuasiveness.

- Highlight all the punctuation used in a continuous prose text in paragraphs (e.g. a page of a novel/magazine article) and in a text organised in a different way (e.g. columns, boxes, bullet points). Record findings in a table and draw some conclusions about punctuation rules and usage.

- Read and discuss some different views on punctuation, recent and not so recent, e.g. from a text book, a guide to usage, a newspaper columnist, a letter to a paper.

See also in the key skills:

Communication key skills level 2
Part A: In reading and summarising information . . .
Part B: C2.2

LEVEL 2

*At this level,
adults can*

read and understand
a range of texts of varying
complexity accurately and
independently

read and obtain information
of varying length and detail from
different sources

in a wide range of text types

Word Focus Vocabulary Rw/L2

Skills, knowledge and understanding

Adults should be taught to:

**① read and understand technical
vocabulary**

– understand that specialist fields of
knowledge, skill and interest have an
associated technical vocabulary

– understand that the purpose of technical
vocabulary is to express precision of meaning

– understand that technical vocabulary is often
coined by adapting/extending the meaning
of existing words and word patterns, or
building new words using known
roots/prefixes/
suffixes and that this can provide clues to
the meaning of unknown words, e.g.
computer menu, astronaut micro-surgery

– understand when it is possible to make an
informed guess at the meaning of technical
vocabulary from knowledge and context and
when it is necessary to look up the meaning
in a dictionary/glossary

**② use reference material to find the
meaning of unfamiliar words**

– understand that there are different sources
of information for word meanings, how they
are structured, and the conventions they use,
e.g. paper and electronic dictionaries,
glossaries, keys

– understand that there are different types of
dictionary, e.g. contemporary usage, slang,
quotations, etymological,
antonyms/synonyms

**③ recognise and understand vocabulary
associated with texts of different levels
of accessibility, formality, complexity and
of different purpose**

– understand that choice of vocabulary
contributes to the style of a text and relates
to context, purpose, audience

– understand how vocabulary clues can be
used to help extract meanings beyond the
literal

– understand the concept of synonyms and that
different words can express similar or related
ideas, qualities, things, often at different
levels of formality

– understand the purpose of, and be able to
use, a thesaurus

– understand that the meaning and use of
some words changes over time and that new
words can be coined

– recognise and understand the use of similes,
metaphors, idioms, clichés

Example

Use knowledge of word roots, word families,
associated connotations and context to work
out the likely meanings of technical words
when encountered for the first time,
e.g. (in a first aid manual) *if the patient is
hyperventilating.*

Look up an unfamiliar word in an appropriate
dictionary and decide from a range of
meanings which one best suits the context,
e.g. when reading a legal letter.

Read a formal text, e.g. a motor insurance
renewal notice, and recognise vocabulary
associated with the subject and with the
formality of a business communication.

Sample activities

- In groups or in a pair, share their own knowledge of technical vocabulary, e.g. in terms of their area of work, cars, computers, a sport or hobby. Compare other learners' technical vocabulary and explain the meaning of their own known words.

- Highlight technical vocabulary used in explanatory texts; decide if it is possible to work out meaning from the word and the context. Check meanings in a dictionary or glossary.

- Choose a new topic of interest, e.g. quilt making, wind surfing, Buddhism. Scan an information text on the chosen subject; note and remember unfamiliar specialist words.

- Use a web-search engine to find information on a topic of interest (e.g. new-generation mobile phones) and find definitions of unfamiliar technical vocabulary. Post what you have discovered on college/work/school bulletin board or conference area.

- Look up words with related roots, and compare information and presentation in an ordinary dictionary and in an etymological dictionary.

- In pairs, identify unfamiliar words in a specialist newspaper or journal report (e.g. on a current economic, environmental, scientific or cultural issue). Decide whether it is possible to make a guess at meanings, looking at the words' structure and context. Make a note of possible meanings. Use a dictionary to check these out, selecting meanings that fit best.

- In a group, play *Call My Bluff*. Each team uses dictionaries to select three or four unfamiliar words, recording definitions. Using knowledge of word roots and origins, invent two more plausible fictitious meanings. Try out words and meanings for the other team to select the most likely.

- When tracing an argument, highlight words or phrases used to link points in the argument, e.g. *certainly, equally, it could be argued, of course, whereas, another possibility, you should, you might.*

- When comparing texts of different degrees of familiarity, identify any idiomatic phrases in informal texts and consider their effects.

- Compare and discuss the use and purpose of similes in a poem and in a promotional text.

- In pairs, explore the use of metaphors in a range of texts, e.g. newspapers, adverts, computer manual, poems; consider their possible origin and decide which are over-worked metaphors that have become clichés.

- Make a personal glossary of interesting words encountered in their own reading; look up their meanings, usage and origins in an appropriate dictionary; use their own glossary for a reference in reading and writing.

- Extend vocabulary by comparing words with a similar meaning. Hold a 'synonyms quiz', where teams research and set questions to ask each other, using a thesaurus, e.g. *How many different words can the team think of to refer to* **walking**? As a follow-on, each team then has five minutes to plan an explanation, to present to the other team, of the differences between all the related terms for that word, and the sorts of context and text where each might occur. This could form part of preparation for writing pieces at different levels of formality or specialism. The activity brings together word-level work, reading to research information, giving and listening to explanations, writing using formal and informal language appropriate to purpose and audience.

*At this level,
adults can*

read and understand
a range of texts of varying
complexity accurately and
independently

read and obtain information
of varying length and detail from
different sources
in a wide range of text types

An example of an integrated activity for reading   **L2**

Teaching focus

Text: how to read an information text with understanding and identify the main points for summarising; how to use different reading strategies at different points in a longer text; how to read critically, taking account of context and sources

Sentence: sentence structure and word order in information-heavy texts; how to use punctuation to help navigate more complicated texts; how to recognise the markers of formal texts, e.g. passive verbs, abstract nouns

Word: specialist terms associated with survey reports; expressions of quantity and qualification

- The text is an extract from a recently published report (one of a series in a study of the family in today's society) on the findings of a survey conducted by MORI for Nestlé to find out what adults aged over 15 in Britain today see as their moral values. 'It does not set out to measure these against any pre-conceived ideas or codes.' (Foreword)

- Introduce the text explaining its context and purpose. Ask learners to spend two minutes scanning the extract to decide what this section appears to be about and how it is organised. Time the two minutes, pool impressions and discuss them, e.g. the numbered heading and its question structure, the use of bullet points rather than continuous text, the use of figures including percentages. Probe if necessary, to see how much of the subject matter they have picked up at this stage, writing up any suggestions.

- In pairs, ask learners to look more closely at the layout of the page, including the different patterns of the left-hand edge, to help them decide how the section might be broken down into sub-sections. They can use up to five horizontal lines to mark off sub-sections; ask them to decide where to put these, drawing them in pencil.

- Then ask learners to look at the last punctuation mark immediately before each of their lines, to circle it and, in view of what each is, decide whether they want to remove or re-position any of their dividing lines. Discuss how people have divided up the text and why, considering the use of bullets, indentation, capital letters, and combinations of these, and of full stops or semi-colons. Look at how some bullets hang off a common stem and form part of a single long sentence, while others are items in a list following a semi-colon. Consider whether this type of layout is easier to follow than continuous text and, if so, why.

- Ask learners individually to read the first sub-section carefully (this will probably be up to *...young people.*), circling any unfamiliar words (e.g. *significant, domain, respondents, perceived*) and underlining any parts that they find hard to follow (possibly the opening sentence and the first bullet point). Discuss possible meanings of the words in context, including the use of *respondents* for people who have taken part in a survey, and the phrase *public domain*. Having looked at difficult words, ask learners if they now understand all the sub-section or if some parts are still hard to follow. This might lead to examination of use of the pronoun *whom* and the phrases *the extent to which, were seen as*, all characteristic expressions of more formal texts and markedly different from everyday spoken language.

- In pairs, ask learners to: locate the sub-section which gives information on the different influences that people said were **most important** to them; highlight key words that explain what those influences are; highlight which influence was rated as important or very important most often by respondents. Discuss findings and consider if they are what learners would have expected, how they would answer if surveyed themselves, the extent to which people tell the truth in surveys, and whether it is possible to include cross-checking questions.

Reproduced with the kind permission of
Société des Produits Nestlé S.A.

4.3 WHO ARE THE MORAL INFLUENCES?

Moral values are considered by many people to be influenced by significant others either in the immediate circle or in the public domain.

We asked two questions about influences;

- the first concerned the people whom our respondents perceived to have influenced them,
- the second concerned the extent to which public figures of today were seen as good or bad influences on young people.

Respondents reported that the most important influences on themselves were

- what their parents told them about right and wrong – 95% placed this as 'important' or 'very important'
- this was followed by the way their family behaved – 91%
- teachers came third at 74% and friends' expectations at 65%
- the way people behaved in radio and television soap operas was least influential, but still rated important by 14%
- characters in books, sportspeople and entertainers, and public figures were seen as influential by about a quarter of the respondents
- perhaps surprisingly, given that only 23% of the respondents described themselves as 'attenders at religious services', 46% rated their religion as an important influence.

There were some quite striking differences amongst groups;

- women rated as more important than did men, the influence of how their family behaved, friends' expectations, and religion, but men rated as more important than women, the influence of the country's rules and laws, and of sportspeople and entertainers.

- Age was as usual a factor;

  the oldest age-group was most influenced by religion, and by rules and laws, and the 25-34 year-olds – least.
  the very young were influenced by characters in soap operas – 27% compared with only 12% of those 55+.

- Religious beliefs were reflected in sources of influence;

  the most devout reported that they were more influenced than were respondents with other degrees of religious affiliation, by religion (unsurprisingly), by particular individuals, by their teachers and by the way their family behaved.

- Personal philosophy, or code for living, also affected perceptions of influences;

  those endorsing 'Love your neighbour as yourself' rated highly what their parents told them about right and wrong, their religion, and particular individuals.

  Those who endorsed 'Always do what you want as long as you don't hurt anyone' gave lower ratings to the influences of what parents told them, the way their family behaved, religion, and the country's rules and laws.

(continued over page)

LEVEL 2 *At this level, adults can*

read and understand
a range of texts of varying
complexity accurately and
independently

read and obtain information
of varying length and detail from
different sources
in a wide range of text types

- Now ask learners to scan to locate differences in what men and women rated highly, and differences between young and old people and to list these points under four column headings: most highly rated by men; most highly rated by women; most highly rated by young people; most highly rated by older people.

- Ask them in pairs (a) to find out what the 'most devout' respondents were influenced by; (b) which of the two 'personal philosophy' statements they themselves would rate more highly.

- Discuss what have emerged as the main points of this section on 'Who are the moral influences?' Consider how best these could be summarised, e.g. in a table, a list, as bullet points, as a spider diagram, as a single paragraph. Ask learners to prepare a summary, specifying a maximum number of words.

Links with speaking, listening and discussion
The text provides subject matter for discussion of quite demanding concepts and ideas, which could begin at a personal level and move to consideration of wider society, requiring learners to express opinions and arguments and to support them with evidence. It could be used, along with other texts on similar or related topics (e.g. from a newspaper, local or national government report, from a popular text book, from a web site), as part of research for a debate on a motion such as *Family and friends are more important influences than the media on present-day behaviour.*

Links with writing
The information reading modelled in this activity can be applied more independently by learners once they have mastered some strategies; it can then be used in conjunction with practising note making and summarising as efficient ways of recording information from reading and organising writing for different purposes. It can also be part of preparation for planning and drafting longer pieces of continuous writing in logical sequences, using formal language.

Writing

Writing is an everyday task

Although the need to write extensively may be limited for many adults, writing nevertheless remains an important form of communication. In everyday life it is difficult to avoid filling in forms; in education and training writing skills are essential, particularly for assessment purposes; and a recent survey into writing in the workplace reported that, although writing was limited in range, scope and variety, it was often of critical importance to the day-to-day business of the organisation and could be crucial to a particular operation or to public image and reputation. But it is not just functional writing that is important; for many adults personal writing is a key to understanding and sharing their experiences. The curriculum provides opportunities for learners to develop writing skills and use these in all aspects of their lives.

Writing tasks

The writing tasks that learners are asked to undertake need to be varied and meaningful, however basic, with an emphasis on communication. Learners need to practise writing at text level even when their grip on individual words is shaky. Otherwise the understanding of the structures of written language, which they have gained through reading, won't be transferred to their own writing.

Learning the language of literacy

Adults are likely to actually welcome learning some of the language of reading and writing. They use specialist vocabulary in other areas of life. If you can talk about gaskets and flues and rotas and shifts and electronic alarm systems, and floats, balances, credit, orders, returns, prescriptions, cash back, log on, mouse, etc, you might feel willing to give verb, noun, subject, phrase, connective, a go. You are then able to talk about and understand the business of organising words into sentences to make meaning.

> I used to sit and watch my wife writing a letter to a friend in America and I used to think "God I wish I could do that", so as soon as I started and I could get it down in writing, that's the first thing I did, I wrote a letter to our friends in America. And I've wrote quite a few since.
>
> from *A Fresh Start – Improving Literacy and Numeracy*, DFEE, 1999

The Sick Rose

O rose, thou art sick!
The invisible worm
That flies in the night,
In the howling storm,

Has found out thy bed
Of crimson joy:
...ark secret love
...life destroy.

Blake

Email

To: Florence Jackson
From: Tina
Subject: Received Mail
Cc:
Bcc:
X-Attachments: None

Dear Florence,

I have been in contact with James Temple recently and have received a letter outlining the costs and structure of new development. I will look into the other matter we talked about last week and will get back to you as soon as I know anything.

Can you please send me your initial quotes on the job as I can compare them with the latest from Mr Williams.

Regards,
Tina.

Letter

Keywood Press
Unit 5
Forrest Ind Estate
Trafford Docks
Manchester
M19 2JD

Bobby S...
15 Upton...
West Di...
Manch...
MB4...

22nd Sept...

Dear Mr Richards,

I would like to apply for the senior printing position advertised in the Daily... newspaper on Thursday 18th September.

I have over five years experience as a printer with the last three years s... operating a five colour Komori. I'm used to dealing with clients first hand a... comfortable with taking briefs and other customer liaison. I have worked o... variety of high profile print jobs meeting tight deadlines always to the va... of standards.

I hope I am what you're looking for and look forward to hearing from you soon.

Yours Sincerely,

B Sordo

V10 Vehicle Licensing Form

Please read the notes overleaf before completing this form
Please write clearly in BLACK INK using CAPITAL LETTERS   95

V10
Official Use Only
Apr/99
Date Stamp

Your Details

Full Name of Vehicle Keeper
Mr/Mrs/Miss/Ms EVANS
Company Name if applicable N/A
Address including postcode 26 WESSEX AVE, COVENTRY
Postcode CY3 1JK

Vehicle Details

Registration mark
Please write clearly in the boxes
(An incorrect or unclear entry could result in further enquiries or an incorrect licence disc being issued) M458 PDF

Taxation class of licence required
(such as private/light goods [PLG]) PLG

If PLG, Bicycle or Tricycle please give exact cylinder capacity 199B (cc)

If bus (ie vehicle with more than 8 passenger seats) or reduced pollution bus state number of seats excluding driver N/A Seats

Make and Model e.g. (Rover 414, Vauxhall Corsa, Ford Mondeo) FORD

Mileage (to the last complete mile) You are not required by law to provide mileage information but doing so may help to prevent mileage fraud

Licence Details

State whether the licence is to run for 6 or 12 months _____ months
There is a 10% surcharge on the cost of a 6 month licence

State date of expiry or surrender of last licence*
If you do not know this because you received the vehicle without a licence give the actual date you received it

State clearly in the boxes, the month and year you want the licence to start*
This must be the first day of the month in which you want the licence to start.

Answer this question if there is a break between the dates marked * above
Has the vehicle been kept (eg parked) or used on a public road at any time between these dates (other than for a pre-arranged compulsory vehicle test)? Answer YES or NO

Keeping or using an unlicensed vehicle on a public road is an offence which could result in a maximum fine of £1...

Declarati...
If the vehicle is a good...
form V112G (see sec...
I declare that I have...
and belief it is correc...
I enclose the paym...

Signature M...

In the case of a partn...

Certificate of Posting

This is a receipt for ordinary letters. Keep it safely to produce in the event of a claim. The ordinary post should not be used for sending money or valuable items.

Royal Mail

Please write the name, address and postcode for each item you're sending in the column below (in ink)

number of items	Officer's initials	date stamp
1	TS	

name MR PETERS
address and postcode 15 ALMA ROAD, LONDON
EC1 1LB

please continue on the back (if necessary)

P326 PAD July 96

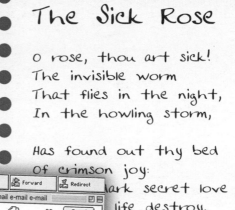

At this level, adults can

write to communicate information to an intended audience

in documents such as forms, lists, messages, notes, records

Text Focus **Writing composition** **Wt/E1**

Skills, knowledge and understanding

Adults should be taught to:

① use written words and phrases to record or present information

– understand that writing is a way of representing language in a more permanent form than speech

– understand that writing can be structured in different ways for different contexts and audiences, e.g. in sentences, in a list

– understand that writers have to plan and organise their thoughts before writing them down

Example

Compose simple texts for themselves and others, e.g. a shopping list, a note to a friend or family.

Sentence Focus **Grammar and punctuation** **Ws/E1**

Skills, knowledge and understanding

Adults should be taught to:

① construct a simple sentence

– understand that writing is not simply speech written down but has its own structures and conventions

– understand the concept of a sentence as the basic building block of continuous written text

Example

Construct grammatically correct simple sentences about themselves and familiar situations, e.g. *My name is Charlie. My bus was late.*

② punctuate a simple sentence with a capital letter and a full stop

– understand that the beginning of a sentence is marked by a capital letter, and the end is marked by a full stop

– understand that writers use these rules to mark off one sentence 'block' from another, which helps the reader follow the text

– understand that a line of writing is not necessarily the same as a sentence

– know and understand the terms, *sentence, capital letter, full stop*

Construct a grammatically correct simple sentence with an initial capital and a full stop, and begin using initial capitals and full stops to mark sentences when writing texts of more than one sentence in their own writing, e.g. in a note to a family member.

③ use a capital letter for personal pronoun 'I'

– understand that the letter 'I' on its own is a word as well as a letter

– understand that the letter 'I' is always spelt with a capital when used for the personal pronoun

– understand that the letter 'I' is often used at the beginning of a sentence

Compose a few sentences about themselves using the capital 'I' for the personal pronoun, e.g. *I am five feet ten tall. I have brown eyes. I have not too much hair left now. I take size eleven shoes.*

Sample activities

- Think of situations where it would be useful to record things, e.g. a note for a workmate coming on the next shift, a note of the date/time of a doctor's appointment, a list of things to pack for a journey. Practise writing these down, with help if necessary.

- List some key autobiographical facts and observations in order to compose a 'pen portrait' of themselves. Help their teacher to write down the account.

- Identify some friends/family members/fellow learners to write to. Choose appropriately illustrated cards/notelets to suit each person from a selection provided by their teacher, and write simple messages on them.

- Compose a simple text message for a mobile phone, e.g.: *Will be home at 8; Give me a call today.*

Content

Planning content is a skill that needs to be taught and learned. Language experience is the starting point for beginning writers (those who lack the technical skills for independent writing), where the teacher produces a written version of the learner's spoken language. Learners can also dictate to tape for later transcription. Discussing work with the teacher lays the foundation of skills in planning, drafting and reviewing, which will be developed over time.

Sample activities

- Practise sentence awareness in games/exercises with their teacher and other learners:

  (a) Compose different simple sentences to express the same idea, e.g. *My name is Charlie./I am called Charlie. I am 42 years old./I was 42 last birthday. I have a son called Mark./Mark is my son.*

  (b) Play 'guess the object/place/person' with their teacher and other learners; the person thinking of an object must only use complete sentences, e.g. *It has a lot of skyscrapers. It has big yellow taxis. Its nickname is the Big Apple.*

  (c) Tell a communal story from a given title; each person adds a complete sentence until a suitable conclusion is reached.

- Look at three linked illustrations/diagrams. Compose a complete sentence to label each one; write down the sentences, with help if necessary, using an initial capital and full stop for each.

- Use a word processor to add initial capitals at the beginning of sentences in someone else's writing.

- Use a word processor to divide a short text into complete sentences by inserting full stops and capitals in the right places.

Sentence structure

Beginning writers are not beginning thinkers, and they may experience frustration when attempting to write what they want to say, because of their lack of technical skills. They may be confined to simple sentences in independent writing, but it is better to understand the concept of a sentence as a unit of meaning at this stage, and to write simple sentences correctly, before progressing to compound and complex sentences. More advanced writers may need to 'go back to basics' with work on simple sentences in order to build up an understanding of sentence structure and to put right misconceptions.

- Proof-read a piece of writing (their own or someone else's) on paper or screen, and change all lower-case personal pronoun 'i's to upper case.

- Use a word processor with the capitalising facility switched on to see how the personal pronoun 'I' is capitalised automatically when typed in lower case.

- Using a 'Cluedo'-style case study, select a character and compose and write an alibi for them, e.g. *I was at the cinema with my boyfriend. I left at 10.30. I went straight home.*

 *At this level, adults can*

write to communicate
information to an intended audience

in documents such as forms, lists, messages, notes, records

 Spelling and handwriting **Ww/E1**

Skills, knowledge and understanding

Adults should be taught to:

❶ spell correctly some personal key words and familiar words

– understand that, to be written down, words have to be spelt

– understand that spelling is rule governed: the same word is always spelt in the same way

– understand how letters are formed and used to spell words

– understand that there are different strategies for learning to spell

– understand that spelling is only one aspect of the writing process

❷ write the letters of the alphabet using upper and lower case

– understand that letters can be written in upper and lower case

– understand that choice of case will vary with context and purpose

❸ use basic sound–symbol association to help spelling, *as appropriate for the needs of the learner*

– understand that sounds are associated with letters and strings of letters

– understand that there are more sounds (phonemes) in English than letters of the alphabet, so some sounds are represented by combinations of letters

– understand that there are many common letter patterns that can be learnt to help spelling

– understand that, to learn to spell, it is important to develop an awareness of sound patterns

– know how to identify and segment phonemes in words for spelling

– understand the terms *vowel* and *consonant*

Example

Spell some personal and familiar words correctly in their own writing (in lists, simple forms, notes to family and friends), e.g.:

• their own name and address

• other important personal words such as the names of their children, their employer

• high-frequency words from the Dolch list (see p.59)

• the days of the week

• numbers to ten.

Write their own name and address correctly in upper case and lower case with initial capitals as required on a form.

Hear, identify and write initial and final phonemes in consonant–vowel–consonant (CVC) words, initial and final consonant phonemes, short medial vowel sounds, e.g. *mug, bet, hit.*

Hear and segment initial consonant clusters, e.g. *bl, st,* and final consonant clusters, e.g. *nd, lp.*

Consonant digraphs, e.g. *ch* (as in *chip), sh, th.*

Sample activities

- In the context of their own composition, practise spelling personal and high-frequency familiar words, using Look, Say, Cover, Write, Check, 'words within words', tracing letters in the air, and other visual and kinaesthetic strategies appropriate to their own learning style.

- Use a word processor to write names, dates and places for captions for a photograph album and print them out.

- Practise spelling key words for simple messages, e.g. days, times, numbers, words from the Dolch list. Use them to write down messages from their teacher/other learners such as when and where to meet up, the day and time of a dental appointment, a message for the milkman/postman.

- Write down letters in response to letter names.

- Practise writing individual letters in upper and lower case on paper and screen.

- Practise writing letters in their own name and address in upper and lower case on paper and screen.

- Complete some personal details on different forms, in upper and lower case, e.g. their name, their address.

- Enter names of friends and family into the 'Names and Numbers' list on a mobile phone, using upper and lower case.

- Practise linking sound and spelling patterns by generating families of rhyming CVC word. In pairs, compose a short rap/comic sound poem orally and share it with their teacher/group, e.g. *Slim Jim he's so thin the doctor's told him he must drink gin; Fat Mat he kick the cat, that cat gone hit him with a cricket bat.*

Phonics and spelling

- recognise all initial consonant and short vowel sounds in speech and writing

- recognise consonant digraphs *sh, ch, th*

- identify and write correct initial letters in response to the letter sound, word, object or picture

- recognise and name each letter of the alphabet and be aware of alphabetical order

- discriminate, write and read final sounds in simple words

- discriminate, write and read middle (short vowel) sounds in simple words: – *a (hat), e (bet), i (lit), o (not), u (mug)*

- read and spell words ending in *ck, ff, ll, ss, ng*

- discriminate, blend and spell initial consonant clusters taken as needed from the following list: *bl, br, cl, cr, dr, dw, fl, fr, gl, gr, pl, pr, sc, scr, sk, sl, sm, sn, sp, spl, spr, squ, st, str, sw, tw, tr, thr, shr*

- discriminate, blend and spell common end clusters, taken as needed from the following list: *ld, nd, lk, nk, sk, lp, mp, sp, ct, ft, lt, nt, pt, st, xt, lf, nch, lth*

- In pairs, invent comic captions orally, using rhyme or another sound pattern for pictures of sports/TV/film celebrities (e.g. *He has a good life with his wife Posh Spice; One spank from Frank and you're flat as a plank,* etc).

- Listen to a tape of rhyming CVC words in short sentences; identify the sound patterns and write down the words.

- In pairs or in a group, think of some words beginning with the same consonant clusters and write them. Try making up a sentence/jingle using some of the words, e.g. *blob, blab, blip, black, blink, blank: Don't blab if you see the black blob. Just blink.* – then say it as quickly as possible.

- Use a text-to-speech program to input and hear CVC words.

At this level, adults can

write to communicate
information with some awareness
of the intended audience

in documents such as forms, lists,
messages, notes, records,
e-mails, simple narratives

Text Focus **Writing composition** **Wt/E2**

Skills, knowledge and understanding

Adults should be taught to:

**❶ use written words and phrases to
record or present information**

– understand the concept of 'fitness for
purpose' in composition – that the writer
selects the best organisation and style for
the context, audience and purpose,
e.g. continuous text/chart/numbered points

Example

Compose and write some short texts for
different audiences in their own daily life,
e.g. an e-mail message to a teacher; an
absence note to a child's teacher; a diary
entry, or a personal reading record; a chart to
record when their child has been given
medicine.

Sentence Focus **Grammar and punctuation** **Ws/E2**

Skills, knowledge and understanding

Adults should be taught to:

**❶ construct simple and compound
sentences, using common
conjunctions to connect two clauses
(e.g. *as, and, but*)**

– understand that simple sentences can be
combined to make compound sentences by
using conjunctions

– understand that, if a compound sentence
has too many bits added on, the reader will
not be able to follow the sense

– know some common conjunctions e.g. *and,
but, or, as*

Example

Compose a letter to a friend or family
member, writing in complete sentences and
using a variety of sentence patterns.

❷ use adjectives

– understand that adjectives extend the
information in sentences, by providing
some detail about a noun

– understand that adjectives help the writer
to describe people, feelings, places,
situations, objects in more detail

– understand that the choice of adjectives
can often convey a writer's attitude

– know and use the term *adjective*

Write a short description of a favourite place
for someone who has not been there.

Sample activities

- Exchange e-mails with a teacher/other learners.

- Use pictures (prepared from a catalogue/birthday cards/sticker books) to plan and write a simple story for a small child.

- Write some short instructions to accompany symbols/illustrations, e.g. on how to use a household product. Ask other learners to check them for ease of use; then try turning the instructions into a flow chart or diagram.

- Choose a topic from their own experience which others do not know much about, e.g. line dancing, some voluntary work, embroidery, horse racing. Compose a 'beginner's guide'. Decide the best way to organise (e.g. in sentences, as a chart, list of points under headings) and present at least three pieces of information for a complete beginner. Try these out on others.

Sample activities

- In pairs or in a group, compose four simple sentences, e.g. on an event in the day's news; write them out leaving a line between each. Discuss how to combine four into two, by selecting the best linking words from a selection provided on cards. Copy the selected words in the right place and adjust the punctuation. Copy out the two new compound sentences with correct full stops and initial capitals.

Sentence structure

Learners need to develop their knowledge of conjunctions and other connectives to avoid repetition, for example through overuse of *and*, *then*, *next* in chronological writing. They also need to understand the use of conjunctions and other connectives in developing arguments, e.g. *if . . . then; so; finally.*

- Using the same four sentences, try to combine all four into one sentence with linking words.

- In pairs, sort six prepared simple sentences on cards into a meaningful sequence. Select linking words to combine some into compound sentences; experiment with the best way to do this. Copy out the new text with the sentence boundaries correctly marked.

- On a word processor, experiment with substituting different adjectives in a text. For example, use the 'Find and Replace' facility in Word to replace the word *nice* with other adjectives in a short text (e.g. postcard).

- In pairs, try describing some illustrations to each other, e.g. (from a fashion or home decoration magazine) a pink loo, an elegant Victorian marble fireplace, horrible wallpaper. Discuss the effect of different types of adjective and identify which adjectives convey attitudes and/or describe appearance.

ENTRY
2
LEVEL

At this level, adults can

write to communicate
information with some awareness
of the intended audience

in documents such as forms, lists,
messages, notes, records,
e-mails, simple narratives

Sentence Focus | Grammar and punctuation | Ws/E2

Skills, knowledge and understanding

Adults should be taught to:

3 use punctuation correctly
(e.g. capital letters, full stops and
question marks)

– understand that capital letters and end-of-
sentence punctuation cannot be used
arbitrarily, but must mark the grammatical
boundaries of a complete sentence

– understand that punctuation is best
thought about at the stage of composition
and included as the sentences are put
down, rather than added from scratch at
the end

– understand that questions are sentences
that have a different word order from
straightforward statements

– understand that question marks signal to
the reader that the sentence is asking a
question

4 use a capital letter for proper nouns

– understand what is meant by a proper noun

– understand the purpose of marking proper
nouns by an initial capital

Example

Write simple and compound sentences
(including questions), using correctly placed
capitals, full stops and question marks, e.g. in
a letter to a friend enquiring whether they are
coming to visit, and when.

Use initial capitals for proper nouns in their
own writing, e.g. a note to a supervisor at
work, or a form in a newspaper to send off for
a brochure of a resort.

Word Focus | Spelling and handwriting | Ww/E2

Skills, knowledge and understanding

Adults should be taught to:

1 spell correctly the majority of
personal details and familiar common
words

– understand that for most people spelling
has to be learnt

– understand that all learners need a range
of strategies but that some work better for
some people than others

– understand that not all spellings can be
worked out from the sound of the word;
visual strategies are needed as well

– understand that looking carefully at letter
patterns when reading helps remember the
spelling for writing

Example

Extend accurate spelling of personal key
words and familiar words when writing for
their family, friends, workmates (in messages,
notes, e-mails), e.g.:

• the names of family members, friends,
workmates, local places

• more high-frequency words from the
Dolch list (see p.67)

• the months of the year

• numbers up to 20.

Sample activities

- Compose a short text explaining/ describing a process from their own experience for another person, e.g. having their eyes tested, having body parts pierced, losing their way on a journey. Write in complete sentences with initial capitals and appropriate end-of-sentence punctuation. Exchange the text with another learner for reading and checking.

- Turn some given statements into questions on a word processor; compare the results with another learner and discuss the effects on word order. Identify the key question words; punctuate the question versions with question marks.

- Find the question mark in text-messaging facilities. Send text messages that include questions to friends, e.g. *When will I see you again?*

- Use a mobile-phone text-messaging facility to copy or write a short note, using upper-case letters as appropriate.

- Share examples from their own experience of different types of proper noun; devise a chart/list/table to record words and add to this new examples that they find in their own reading.

- Compose some e-mails using a list of proper nouns, e.g. to a TV station to request the return of a programme, to a local radio show asking them to play a friend's favourite track, to a newsagent to order a new magazine.

Sample activities

- In the context of their own writing, practise spelling personal and high-frequency words using a range of spelling strategies appropriate to their own preferred learning style.

- Start a personal spelling dictionary, such as the dictionary facility that exists on some mobile phones. Record unfamiliar spellings in lower-case letters on the appropriate letter page; write a short definition alongside it if necessary. Use it for reference in their own writing.

- Group the months of the year into those with similar spelling patterns and discuss the origins of the names with their teacher and other learners. Write out the correct full spelling for each month alongside their abbreviated and numerical forms. Use Look, Say, Cover, Write, Check to learn.

- Complete their personal details, correctly spelt on a variety of simple forms.

At this level, adults can

write to communicate
information with some awareness
of the intended audience

in documents such as forms, lists,
messages, notes, records,
e-mails, simple narratives

| Word Focus | Spelling and handwriting | Ww/E2 |

Skills, knowledge and understanding

Adults should be taught to:

2 use their knowledge of sound–symbol
relationships and phonological patterns
(e.g. consonant clusters and vowel
phonemes) to help work out correct
spellings, *as appropriate for the needs of
the learner*

  – understand that many words follow regular
    spelling patterns which correspond to
    certain sounds
  – understand that it is possible to greatly
    reduce the chances of making random
    spelling errors by applying their knowledge
    of spelling patterns and rules
  – understand that adding *–s* to nouns is a
    common way of indicating more than one,
    and know the term *plural*
  – understand that *–ed* and *–ing* are common
    spellings at the end of words to show the
    past and present forms of verbs
  – understand that some words can be split
    into parts to help spelling, e.g. compound
    words, words with prefixes or suffixes

3 produce legible text
  – understand the concept of 'fitness for
    purpose' in the presentation of writing,
    e.g. that the critical importance of accuracy,
    legibility, neatness will vary depending on
    context, audience and purpose
  – understand that handwriting and word
    processing are skills that people need to
    learn to use to produce legible text in
    different circumstances

Example

Extend and secure their knowledge of the
spelling of common regular words, including:

- common spelling patterns for long vowel
  phonemes (see opposite);
- common spelling patterns for vowel
  phonemes (see opposite);
- plurals ending in *–s*
- verbs with *–ed* and *–ing* endings
- familiar compound words, e.g. *football,
  teaspoon*
- words with common prefixes, e.g. *un–,
  dis–,* to indicate the negative.

Record some important information, in a work
context, in a clearly legible and intelligible
form on paper or screen, e.g. goods received,
a product tracking record, a machine service
record, information to update next shift.

Sample activities

- Listen to a tape of short sentences containing missing words with the same vowel phonemes. After each sentence, write down the word indicated by the tape, applying their knowledge of likely spellings which can represent that sound.

- Using words from their own spelling dictionary or another familiar text, identify with their teacher/other learners which words can have a meaningful plural form. Draw up some rules.

- Identify a list of nouns from their own reading/writing and write down their plural forms. Check this with the teacher/other learners.

- Assess their own handwriting style with their teacher for legibility and fluency. Identify what aspects need improvement, e.g. letter spacing, sizing, orientation. Practise their handwriting, in conjunction with spelling and independent writing.

- Work through a systematic handwriting improvement plan if they wish.

- Use a word processor to write something that should preferably be printed, e.g. captions for photographs, instructions, a notice.

- Use the 'Format: Change Case' facility to compare texts in all upper or all lower case.

- Apply different fonts and sizes to a short text to compare their readability and suitability.

Phonics and spelling

Discriminate, spell and read the common spelling patterns for the long vowel phonemes: *ee, ai, ie, oa, oo*

ee:	*ee (feet)*	*ea (seat)*		
ai:	*ai (train)*	*a–e (name)*	*ay (play)*	
ie:	*ie (lie)*	*i–e (bite)*	*igh (high)*	*y (fly)*
oa:	*oa (boat)*	*o–e (pole)*	*ow (show)*	
oo:	*oo (moon)*	*u–e (tune)*	*ew (flew)*	*ue (blue)*

Discriminate, spell and read the common spelling patterns for the vowel phonemes: *oo, ar, oy, ow*

oo:	*u (pull)*	*oo (good)*
ar:	*ar (car)*	
oy:	*oi (boil)*	*oy (boy)*
ow:	*ow (cow)*	*ou (sound)*

Discriminate, spell and read the common spelling patterns for the vowel phonemes: **air, or, er**

air: *air (fair)   are (scare)   ere (there)   ear (bear, wear)*

or: *or (sport)   oor (floor)   aw (claw)   au (caught)   ore (more, store)*

er: *er (her, were)   ir (bird)   ur (fur)*

Discriminate, spell and read the common spelling patterns for the vowel phonemes: **ear, ea**

ear:	*ear (fear, hear)*
ea:	*ea (bread, head)*

Handwriting

The physical process of writing can be extremely laborious for some learners and can inhibit writing as communication. Learners can develop skills in composition using alternative tools, and focus separately on handwriting. Ultimately, however, the only way to improve legibility and speed is practice. As with spelling, grammar and punctuation, learners need to consider when legibility is important (it might be argued that all writing needs to be legible, but most of us can read our own handwriting, even if no-one else can, and that's good enough for a shopping list, or a personal reminder).

Where necessary, learners need to be taught how to form letters, both small letters and capitals, and how to join letters. Handwriting practice can be combined initially with spelling. Learners also need to practise writing in limited spaces, such as on forms.

At this level, adults can

write to communicate
information and opinions with some adaptation to the intended audience

in documents such as forms, notes, records, e-mails, letters, narratives, simple instructions, short reports

 Text Focus | **Writing composition** | **Wt/E3**

Skills, knowledge and understanding

Adults should be taught to:

1 plan and draft writing

– understand that the choice of how to organise writing depends on the context and audience

– understand that there are different ways of planning, e.g. notes to organise and review thinking, a list of points to include, a diagram to group related points together

– understand that drafting follows planning and involves turning plans into something nearer the finished version

– understand that some writing has to be written straight off, with the only planning taking place in the writer's head

2 organise writing in short paragraphs

– understand that paragraphs normally consist of more than one sentence

– understand that paragraphs are not arbitrary divisions put in at the end of writing but a way of grouping the main points and supporting detail at the drafting stage

– understand that paragraphs are often introduced by a topic sentence

– understand that paragraphs can be arranged under headings in certain sorts of texts, e.g. information texts

– understand that paragraphs need to follow on from each other using appropriate linking words

3 sequence chronological writing

– understand that some writing is sequenced by order of events in time

– understand that certain linking words are useful to join sentences and paragraphs in chronological writing, e.g. *first, then, later, while, before, after*

4 proof-read and correct writing for grammar and spelling

– know when to proof-read, i.e. after drafting and editing, to check if the text can be the final version

Example

Plan and draft their own writing to a satisfactory final standard for the task, e.g. a letter to a teacher explaining they are going on holiday; a story or poem for a college or community magazine.

Plan, draft and write a continuous coherent text of at least half a page divided into short paragraphs, e.g. a description of a place for the opening of a story/novel, a reply to a business letter received at home.

Write the chronological account of a recent event in their own life, e.g. going to see their child in a school concert.

Write the description of a process where stages must occur in a particular sequence, e.g. preparing a wall and hanging wall paper.

Proof-read their own writing, on paper and screen, identifying and correcting the main errors of sense and spelling; use a dictionary/spell check if necessary.

Sample activities

- Following a discussion with their teacher/other learners, plan the main points to go in a guide for new learners enrolling on the course.

- Fill in a pre-prepared outline of a spider diagram or mind map with key points to be included in their own writing, e.g. for an A4 information sheet on a topic of their own interest.

- Using a real situation or case study, plan and draft a letter of enquiry on a word processor. Share the draft with their teacher/other learner and take account of their comments at the next stage.

- In pairs or in a group, identify a subject of concern on which to write a memo (e.g. to the council about the shortage of local parking/public transport); pool some ideas. Plan and organise points using their own preferred method; draft three short paragraphs drawing on some pre-identified opening sentences and a list of linking words as necessary. Share with other learners; write out final version.

- Using notes on information obtained from their reading (e.g. on a holiday destination), identify a heading and sub-headings under which to write up their findings. Draft some short paragraphs to expand the headings and write up.

- Explore the features of chronological writing by sequencing some given sentences on a word processor (e.g. describing a process or an event) using the 'Edit: Cut and Paste' facilities. Compare their own version with other learners'.

- Plan and draft a short report of an incident, presenting the events in the order that they occurred.

- In pairs, each proof-read and correct their own writing. Read once for sense (and to point out where the meaning is not clear) and once for spelling mistakes; correct as necessary.

- Practise proof-reading and correcting their own writing, some of which has been handwritten, some of which has been written on a word processor. Discuss and compare the processes.

- Use the 'Tools: Spelling' facility in Word to check their writing.

- Edit a short text message sent in upper case on a mobile phone, entering correct spelling and lower case, and adding full stops and punctuation where required. Send the message to teacher/learner/friends/family.

Purpose and audience

The purpose of writing influences content, format and style. The audience influences content, style and accuracy.

Pre-set formats

The format of text is determined by purpose and convention. Certain types of document – such as telephone message pads, cheques, forms – have pre-set formats, and learners need practice in understanding and using the given format.

Support for writing

Writing frames are a way of providing learner writers with a support or 'scaffold' to help them develop independent skills for different types of writing, e.g.: some headings, subheadings and connectives for linking paragraphs when writing an explanatory information text; the layout, salutation, opening sentence and closure when practising a letter; sentence openings for making contrasting points when presenting an argument.

To be used effectively writing frames need to:

(a) offer enough support to help the learner attempt a new or difficult task, but not so much that the writing is reduced to filling in boxes, which will provide no scope for the learner to improve – the writing frame must require the learner to produce independent continuous text, at the appropriate level;

(b) be used as part of the planning and drafting stages, helping learners marshal their thoughts and organise what they want to write;

(c) be properly structured to suit the type of text and style of writing being practised – a frame for a description will be different from one for some instructions;

(d) be designed and used progressively, providing less scaffolding for harder tasks as learners gain in experience and skill;

(e) be used alongside reading texts that model the type of writing being practised.

Used in this way, writing frames can help learners to extend their repertoire of writing genres, learn the requirements of more formal registers, and improve the cohesiveness of their writing – all of which makes them more able to tackle different writing tasks independently in their own lives.

At this level, adults can

write to communicate
information and opinions with
some adaptation to the intended
audience

in documents such as forms,
notes, records, e-mails, letters,
narratives, simple instructions,
short reports

Sentence Focus   **Grammar and punctuation**   **Ws/E3**

Skills, knowledge and understanding

Adults should be taught to:

① write in complete sentences

- understand that simple and compound
  sentences can be amplified by expanding
  the information around the noun and the
  verb to give additional information about
  agents and actions

- understand that longer or more complicated
  sentences are built up according to
  patterns or rules, relating to word order

**② use correct basic grammar
   (e.g. appropriate verb tense,
   subject–verb agreement)**

- understand the concepts of past, present
  and future, that human beings exist in time,
  and that language reflects this through the
  tenses of verbs which can change form to
  convey time past, present or future

- understand that verbs convey actions
  (physical and non-physical)

- understand that a verb and its subject or
  'doer' must 'agree'; both must be either
  singular (i.e. one) or plural (i.e. more than one)

- understand that in some regional varieties of
  spoken English the subject and verb do not
  always agree (e.g. *we was, he were*) but, as
  written English is a non-regional standard,
  writers use the same written forms wherever
  they live

- know and understand the terms *verb,
  tense, subject of a sentence*

**③ use punctuation correctly (e.g. capital
   letters, full stops, question marks,
   exclamation marks)**

- understand that these are the complete
  family of sentence boundary markers used
  in continuous text written in complete
  sentences

- understand that exclamation marks and
  sometimes question marks can affect
  meaning, and can act as the equivalent of
  intonation in spoken language

Example

Use complete sentences, both simple and
compound, in everyday written
communication.

Write grammatically correct sentences using
the past, present and future tense as needed,
with subject–verb agreement, e.g. a report to
a community group, a letter to their child's
school.

Write an informal letter or account of an
experience using complete sentences marked
with capital letters, full stops, question marks
and exclamation marks as appropriate.

Sample activities

- In pairs or in a group, work on a short narrative written in simple and compound sentences; discuss and annotate to experiment with how detail might be added, e.g. by adjectives and adjectival phrases and adverbials of time, place. Write out extended text in complete sentences, e.g. the text *The man walked down the street and sat on the bench. He took out a newspaper and read it. He put his head in his hands.* might become *Early one Sunday morning the grey-haired old man walked slowly down the empty street. He sat down heavily on the wooden bench. From his pocket he took out a crumpled newspaper and read it carefully. Suddenly he put his head in his bony hands.*

- Practise writing instructions, e.g. for a piece of household/DIY equipment/game/sport in complete sentences, for other learners, using a writing frame if necessary. Ask another person to check the finished version for clarity.

- Send a formal note by fax or e-mail (or something similar) to a friend/work colleague to confirm, e.g. a meeting, purchase order, or similar. Check that complete sentences are used.

- Write a grammatically correct narrative or recount of their own experience in the simple past tense.

- Identify when things might need to be written in the present tense, where the subject is on-going, e.g. as in a notice, instructions, the description of a local habitat for wildlife developed by a community environmental project. Complete a writing task which requires the present tense, using a writing frame for support if necessary.

- In pairs, practise identifying subject and verb 'partners' in sentences in continuous text by highlighting pairs in the same colour. Label pairs as singular or plural and discuss the different forms and endings.

- In pairs, compose some sentences that could be punctuated with a full stop, question mark or exclamation mark, depending on the meaning required, e.g. *She fired the gun. She fired the gun? She fired the gun!* Discuss the differences in meaning and use this to compose appropriate follow-on sentences for each alternative.

- With teacher and other learners, identify and discuss a subject on which people have strong views. Each write the text of a short speech, in complete sentences, using a writing frame if necessary and putting forward a minimum of three points; the speeches must include at least one question and one exclamation correctly punctuated. Everyone reads out their own speech, using punctuation to guide delivery.

- Write a note to put through a friend's door arranging to meet in a particular place to go and see a particular film/group and visit a particular pub/club afterwards. Use the capital *I*, initial capitals for sentences and proper nouns correctly.

- Insert correct punctuation into an unedited text, using a word processor.

What is grammar?

Grammar is concerned with the structure of a language, the order in which words can be placed to make sense, the types of word and their functions in sentences, and the forms the words can take. It is now widely believed that humans are born with the facility to acquire language and so are able to learn to speak the language they hear around them, absorbing the complexities of its grammar and vocabulary from their earliest years.

Implicit and explicit knowledge

Though speech comes 'naturally' to most humans, we have to be taught to read and write. Being taught some explicit knowledge about how language is put together can help adult learners relate their literacy learning to what they already know implicitly about language. It can make them more conscious of how language works in the texts they read and of how they can manipulate it themselves to express their meanings. It can also provide them with some concepts and terms, some meta-language with which to think and talk about language and their own developing skills.

Language – rule governed not random

Knowing explicitly about, for example, verb tenses, pronouns, uses of conjunctions to link parts of sentences, how paragraphs can be linked, the grammatical characteristics of different types of text helps learners consciously understand that language is not random but rule governed, that, although speakers and writers have choices over certain aspects, these operate within a given structure. The knowledge that there are patterns that can be studied, modelled and learnt can help adults to feel there is some logic to the processes of reading and writing and that, given time and teaching, they can master them.

ENTRY LEVEL 3 *At this level, adults can*

write to communicate
information and opinions with
some adaptation to the intended
audience

in documents such as forms,
notes, records, e-mails, letters,
narratives, simple instructions,
short reports

Word Focus   Spelling and handwriting   Ww/E3

Skills, knowledge and understanding

Adults should be taught to:

❶ spell correctly common words and relevant key words for work and special interest

– know and understand their own preferred strategies for extending spelling competence

– understand the importance of cumulative learning in spelling, of relating new to known spellings

– know that there are dictionaries specifically for spelling, and understand that ordinary dictionaries can be used to check spellings if the initial letters are known

– understand that some special-interest texts have glossaries of terms which can be used as reference for spelling as well as meaning

– understand that a computer spell-checker is of limited use until the user can judge how appropriate the suggested corrections are for the sense

❷ use their developing knowledge of sound–symbol relationships and phonological patterns to help spell a greater range of words and longer words, *as appropriate for the needs of the learner*

– understand that knowing spelling patterns (e.g. common letter strings, visual patterns, analogies) reduces the chance of random errors

– understand that there is not always a strict sound–symbol association in spelling, e.g. silent letters

– understand how segmenting words into phonemes and breaking them into syllables (beats) or components (compounds) helps work out spelling

❸ produce legible text

– understand that handwriting is the most suitable/only medium for some tasks and word processing is preferable for others

– understand the features of a clear, legible handwriting style

Example

Spell correctly key words relating to their work routines, leisure and study.

Apply strategies for working out the likely spelling of words in their own writing from their knowledge of rules and patterns.

Handwrite a legible and reasonably neat letter to a friend or family member.

Sample activities

- Record new key spellings in their own spelling dictionary and learn to spell them.

- Use a spelling dictionary to check the spellings in their own writing.

- In pairs or in a group, make a list of words related to their own work/leisure/special interest. Write down a list, with help if necessary. Identify any common spelling patterns in related terms, e.g. *engine, engineer, engineering; freeze, freezer, frozen*. Write a short explanatory text for other learners, using identified specialist words and spelling them correctly.

- Sort the words in a mobile phone or computer-based personal dictionary into different folders, according to different categories or level of difficulty.

Spelling and word structure

- Use word endings to support reading and spelling, e.g. *–s* (plural), *–ed* (past tense), *–ing* (present tense).

- Change the spelling of a word when adding an ending such as *–ed* (past tense), *–ing* (present tense), *–er, –est*.

- Read and spell words with silent letters, e.g. **knee, knife, gnaw, gnat, wrinkle.**

- Recognise common prefixes such as *un–, dis–, de–, re–, pre–*.

- Use the knowledge of prefixes to generate new words from root words, e.g. **happy/unhappy; appear/disappear.**

- Recognise common suffixes such as *–ful, –ly, –less.*

- Use the knowledge of suffixes to generate new words from root words, e.g. *hope/hopeful/hopeless.*

- Split compound words into component parts for reading and spelling, e.g. *football, himself, underneath, airport, playground.*

- Write a short recount in the past tense applying rules for spelling verbs with *–ed/–d* endings.

- In pairs, generate antonyms for a given list of words by adding prefixes, e.g. *un–, mis–, dis–, in–;* write pairs of words in their personal spelling dictionary for reference in their own writing.

- In pairs, identify comparative and superlative forms for adjectives requiring suffixes; discuss how new forms might be spelt. Look at the correct spellings and work out some rules (e.g. *pale, paler, palest; sad, sadder, saddest).*

- Listen to some unfamiliar words on tape and discuss how they might be spelt, drawing on their existing spelling knowledge (e.g. *frighten* – cf *fright; listening* – cf *listen; playground* – cf *play + ground),* then look at the words written down. Annotate them to emphasise their structure and familiar parts. Record them in their spelling dictionary.

- Use a text-to-speech program to apply a range of prefixes and suffixes to root words. Check the words in Word's Thesaurus.

- Make a handwritten fair copy of a short letter from their own draft composition.

- Write out a favourite recipe by hand or on screen to circulate to other learners.

See also in the key skills:

Communication key skills level 1
Part A: In writing documents . . .
Part B: C1.3

At this level, adults can

write to communicate
information, ideas and opinions clearly using length, format and style appropriate to purpose and audience

in documents such as forms, records, e-mails, letters, narratives, instructions, reports, explanations

 Text Focus **Writing composition** **Wt/L1**

Skills, knowledge and understanding

Adults should be taught to:

① plan and draft writing

- understand that planning must take account of purpose, context and audience

- understand that planning needs to be sufficiently clear and organised to be used as the basis for drafting

- know different techniques for planning writing, e.g. notes, lists, diagrams, flow charts

- know when planning and drafting are appropriate and when it is necessary to write something straight off

② judge how much to write and the level of detail to include

- understand that the length of text and the level of detail depend on the nature of the content and on purpose and audience

- understand that planning and drafting involve making decisions on length and detail

③ present information in a logical sequence using paragraphs where appropriate

- understand that information is best presented so that: the opening clearly signals the subject to the reader; points are organised in a logical order; it is clear how one point relates to another; the whole makes coherent sense

- understand that paragraphs are one way of organising information in continuous text, enabling the main points to be expanded with supporting detail

④ use language suitable for purpose and audience

- understand that writers can select language at different levels of complexity, formality and specialism, and depending on context, audience and purpose

- understand that some types of written communication have specific language associated with them, e.g. invitations, estate agents' leaflets

Example

Plan and draft their own writing where the context requires careful thought, e.g. an 'olive branch' letter to a friend or family member, an article for a community/church/volunteer group/college news-sheet.

Plan, draft and write a speech to be delivered at a family function, e.g. wedding, special birthday.

Plan, draft and write some information or instructions where points are logically sequenced, e.g. a leaflet on the local neighbourhood for newcomers, a notice about the company social club and how to join.

Write different texts using the language appropriate to the form of communication and situation, e.g. an advert to go in a shop window or local paper, a letter of application for a job.

Sample activities

- Discuss alternative planning techniques. Plan some writing on a topic of personal interest using their own preferred method; exchange plans with another learner and compare techniques.

- Plan the key points to be included in an explanation of a familiar process. Draft and review for accuracy and clarity.

Style

Style is about the combination of choices a writer makes – of language, syntax, organisation – influenced by context, purpose, audience. Adult learners are likely to already understand and recognise aspects of style (e.g. levels of formality) in their reading, even if they cannot yet reproduce them. As they read and discuss an increasing range of types of text, their implicit understanding of style will be extended and made more explicit. They can then draw on this knowledge for their own writing. As they experiment with different styles in different types of text, they will bring together text-level work with work at sentence and word level on choices of grammatical structure and vocabulary.

- Share experiences of texts where length/level of detail are not right for the purpose (e.g. some instructions for DIY furniture, fliers through the door where the purpose is not clear, school reports that are too general).

- In pairs, work on different types of task (e.g. writing some instructions, an e-mail to a family member living abroad, a letter of apology). Plan and draft outlines for each, indicating the target length, the main content points and their order. Compare and discuss plans.

- Draft a letter on Word, for example to the head teacher at your child's school. Consider how much to write as text.

- Identify a topic from their own knowledge/interest/reading to write 'an introduction' to (e.g. greyhound racing/yoga/aerobics/weight training/country music). Discuss the key facts people might want to know; plan which points to include and in what order. Share the plan with others and 'tweak' if necessary.

- Use this plan to draft an informal information text addressed directly to the reader, paying attention to its opening and to how one point follows from another (select from a list of linking words and phrases if necessary, e.g. *firstly, secondly, finally, first of all, to sum up, you might think that, as well as, before, after, however, then*, etc.).

- Discuss what factors might influence a writer's decision about the sort of language to use for a task, e.g. how much precision is needed, how much will the reader already know about the subject, how well does the writer know the reader, does the context need tact or directness, is there a point of view to get across? Write two different short texts, e.g. recording the details of a traffic accident for an insurance company, describing a brilliant goal/shot/try/race for a newspaper sports page.

- Write a set of safety instructions for a primary school audience (e.g. on road safety) and for an adult audience (e.g. on the correct use of some dangerous equipment).

- Join an on-line 'chat room' (Computer Mediated Text Conference). Read recent and current 'chats', and respond in the appropriate style.

See also in the key skills: Communication key skills level 1
Part A: In writing documents . . .
Part B: C1.3

At this level, adults can

write to communicate
information, ideas and opinions clearly using length, format and style appropriate to purpose and audience

in documents such as forms, records, e-mails, letters, narratives, instructions, reports, explanations

Text Focus   **Writing composition**   **Wt/L1**

Skills, knowledge and understanding

Adults should be taught to:

5 **use format and structure for different purposes**

– understand that there are different ways of organising and presenting text, depending on its type and purpose, e.g. paragraphs, numbered lists, bulleted points, charts, tables, sub-headings

– understand that diagrams, sketches, drawings can be used alongside writing to make meaning clearer, e.g. instructions, explanations

– understand that a lot of workplace writing uses pre-set and outline formats, e.g. accident report forms, timesheets, job sheets, memo headings

6 **proof-read and revise writing for accuracy and meaning**

– understand that proof-reading is about checking for meaning as well as spelling, and that writing must communicate meaning clearly to the reader

– know and use techniques for proof-reading, to spot errors and omissions in grammar, punctuation and spelling

– understand when complete accuracy is essential and when it is better to get writing 'good enough', and move on to the next task

Example

Select the best format and structure for a purpose in their own writing, e.g. draw a flow chart to arrange some actions into steps.

Proof-read and revise their own writing to correct grammar, punctuation and spelling, locating omissions, repetitions, errors, e.g. in a letter.

Sentence Focus   **Grammar and punctuation**   **Ws/L1**

Skills, knowledge and understanding

Adults should be taught to:

1 **write in complete sentences**

– understand that sentences can be joined with a wider range of conjunctions than *as, and, but*, e.g. *if, so, while, though, since, when* to express meaning more precisely

– understand that complete sentences should not be strung together with commas (comma splicing) to make longer 'sentences', but should be split into separate sentences or be correctly joined, e.g. by a conjunction

Example

Use a range of different sorts of complete sentence in their own writing to suit the text type, audience and purpose, e.g. in a letter to a child, to a friend, to an organisation.

Sample activities

- Using a word processor, design a poster to advertise a local event.

- Plan, structure and set out appropriately on paper or screen a 'personal manifesto', e.g. announcing a set of 'house rules' to the family, setting out some new year resolutions/promises to themselves or others/plans for a healthier lifestyle/a 'wish list' for the future.

- Discuss with their teacher and other learners the level of correctness needed in different pieces of their own writing.

- Practise proof-reading their own writing on paper by highlighting/annotating and correcting errors, omissions, repetitions to clarify meaning, on a photocopy of the original. Judge if the revisions to sense are minor and can be made easily, or whether a new fair copy will have to be made.

- Proof-read and make revisions, using 'cut and paste' if necessary to writing saved on the computer. Use the spell check carefully, making sure any changes are the right ones by reading for sense first.

Sample activities

- Using a text written in simple sentences (e.g. the stages in a process such as starting up a car engine, applying a decorative paint effect to a door), experiment with different ways of combining the sentences into longer ones while still keeping the same sense. Compare the two versions.

End-of-sentence punctuation

Too often, learners are taught that full stops and commas correspond to pauses in spoken language. But the sentences of spoken language do not follow the same rules as written sentences. End-of-sentence punctuation needs to be taught in the context of developing a 'sense of sentence', that is, learning to recognise what comprises a complete grammatical *written* sentence.

- Learn to recognise sentence boundaries when proof-reading their own writing by looking for where a new idea or action begins. If this is not marked as a new sentence, place a ruler on its edge between the end of one idea/action and the next. Read the parts of the sentence on either side and decide if each is a complete sentence; if it is, add a full stop and initial capital letter, or see how the two parts can be properly joined, e.g.

Most football hooligans have jobs and plenty of money, they could not travel abroad if they did not, people think they are all young lads, they are not, they are often aged thirty to forty.

could become

Most football hooligans have jobs and plenty of money because they could not travel abroad if they did not. People think they are all young lads but they are not. They are often aged thirty to forty.

- Work from notes made as the result of a discussion, reading passage or video (stored on Notepad or other on-line notes facility). Edit the notes to make sure that complete sentences are used.

See also in the key skills: Communication key skills level 1
Part A: In writing documents . . .
Part B: C1.3

LEVEL 1   *At this level, adults can*

write to communicate information, ideas and opinions clearly using length, format and style appropriate to purpose and audience

in documents such as forms, records, e-mails, letters, narratives, instructions, reports, explanations

Sentence Focus   Grammar and punctuation   Ws/L1

Skills, knowledge and understanding

Adults should be taught to:

❷ use correct grammar (e.g. subject–verb agreement, correct use of tense)

– understand that, while writing, a writer needs to keep checking that singular subjects have a singular verb and that plural subjects have a plural verb

– understand that it is easy to change tense unintentionally while writing and it is important to check for the correct tense

Example

Write grammatically correct sentences with subject–verb agreement and the correct use of tense over a text of at least one paragraph or equivalent, e.g. the account of an experience.

❸ punctuate sentences correctly, and use punctuation so that meaning is clear

– know all the punctuation markers for the beginnings and ends of sentences, and know when to use each one

– understand that, in writing which is not in sentences, other punctuation can be used to make meaning clear, e.g. colons to mark the start of a list, dashes before each item in a vertical list

Write a letter to someone they do not know personally with correct use of capital letters and end-of-sentence punctuation.

Word Focus   Spelling and handwriting   Ww/L1

Skills, knowledge and understanding

Adults should be taught to:

❶ spell correctly words used most often in work, studies and daily life

– know and apply a range of methods (visual, phonetic, kinaesthetic, use of analogies and mnemonics) to help learn and remember correct spellings

– know and apply some spelling rules to help attempt and check spellings (see opposite)

– understand that the spelling of homophones is related to meaning and grammar

Example

Use strategies to attempt and check spellings with confidence in their own writing.

Recognise when it is necessary to double-check a spelling, e.g. by using their own personal spelling or another dictionary, by asking another person.

❷ produce legible text

– understand the different aspects relating to legible text written by hand and by word processor

– understand that a word processor is an ideal tool to use where presentation is very important (e.g. a CV) because it allows errors to be corrected without evidence of the alterations

Handwrite a legible and neatly presented letter to someone outside the family.

Sample activities

- Work in pairs to help develop grammatical awareness and apply it when writing, e.g. stop every 10 minutes, get to the end of the next sentence, read out their own writing to their partner to check for grammatical sense and correctness. Alternatively, exchange their writing with their partner, read each other's writing and discuss its sense.

- Develop an awareness of different verb tenses by rewriting short extracts in a different tense, e.g. a paragraph of an autobiography, a report on a current issue, an advertisement for a holiday. Discuss the effect of changing the tense on other words, word order, the meaning of the text as a whole.

- Use word processor to change verbs from present to past, or to change nouns and verbs from singular to plural.

- Reinforce their understanding of punctuation as part of the writing process by using 'punctuation spot checks' with a partner. When composing a piece of writing in continuous text, one member of the pair says 'Stop!' Writers at once exchange texts and proof-read each other's to check if punctuation is being used. Discuss their findings.

- Plan, draft and write a short narrative or description to be marked specifically for sentence punctuation and capital letters, which they highlight to show up clearly for their teacher.

Commas

Commas can be problematic because they have several uses, but most importantly learners need to know where they should NOT be used – that is, where a full stop or other end-of-sentence marker is needed. The use of commas to separate items in a list is relatively straightforward. Commas to separate clauses or to bracket off a phrase need to be taught in the context of developing control of complex sentences, while drawing attention to their use in various text types.

Spelling and word structure

- Spell two-syllable words containing double consonants, e.g. *muddle, kettle, common* and understand rules for doubling consonants with suffixes.

- Identify and spell irregular verb forms, e.g. *would, could, should.*

- Understand spelling patterns in plurals, using rules such as:
  - when *y* is preceded by a consonant, change *y* to *i* and add *–es, e.g. lady/ladies;*
  - when *y* is preceded by a vowel, add *–s,* e.g. *key/keys;*
  - add *–es* to most words ending in *–s, –sh, –ch,* e.g. *church/churches;*
  - change *–f* to *–ves,* e.g. *thief/thieves.*

- Read and spell suffixes such as: *–al, –ary, –ship, –ness, –ible, –able, –tion, –sion.*

Sample activities

- Use spelling strategies and dictionaries to check spelling as part of the standard proof-reading process with their own writing.

- In a group, each person gives a new word that they have needed to be able to spell since the last class; anyone can volunteer to spell it; if they cannot, the teacher writes the correct spelling on the flipchart; learners select which words to add to their personal dictionary.

- Take a list of common homophones/near homophones (e.g. *their/there/they're, hear/here, where/were/we're, you're/your, of/off, to/two/too)* and in a pair compose a comical text which uses each word correctly, e.g. *The bouncers dust down their suits. There are six of them on the door and they're all very tough. You can hear them down the street calling, 'Get out of here. Where do you think you're going to?' 'We're coming in.' 'No, you're not. Take your mate with you and the two of you push off. You lot can go with them too.'* Then discuss what they learn from this exercise about the various words, e.g. their forms, how they can be used, the sort of writing they could be used for, and their meanings.

- Plan, draft and handwrite a short text to entertain (e.g. a poem, the opening of a story, a comical anecdote) and exchange texts with their partner to read.

- Identify a writing task where legibility and neatness are essential (e.g. a letter of application for a job) and use a word processor to compose, draft and edit it to produce legible text.

See also in the key skills: Communication key skills level 2
Part A: In writing documents . . .
Part B: C2.3

LEVEL 2 *At this level, adults can*

write to communicate
information, ideas and opinions clearly and effectively, using length, format and style appropriate to purpose, content and audience

in a wide range of documents

 Writing composition   Wt/L2

Skills, knowledge and understanding   **Example**

Adults should be taught to:

1 **plan and draft writing**

– understand that planning and drafting include sub-stages:

(a) organising information and thinking in note/diagram form

(b) distinguishing what *must* go in from what *might* go in, and deciding the optimum length for the task

(c) choosing the appropriate language and structure to get across their meaning

– understand that planning and drafting decisions relate to the subject matter, type of text, purpose and audience

Plan and draft a report to present at a community meeting.

Plan and draft an assignment for studies.

2 **judge how much to write and the level of detail to include**

– understand that the length of text and the level of detail depend on the nature of the content and on purpose and audience

– understand that planning and drafting involve making decisions on length and detail

Plan, draft and write a formal letter providing the necessary level of information.

3 **present information and ideas in a logical or persuasive sequence, using paragraphs where appropriate**

– understand that how material is best sequenced will depend on the type of content and purpose of writing, e.g.:

(a) in explanation or description, the writer should consider whether the reader needs to understand certain points before they can understand others (e.g. how a car engine works)

(b) in persuasive texts, the writer needs to sequence information and ideas in the way most likely to convince the reader (e.g. to use public transport in favour of cars)

(c) some writing needs to combine both techniques (e.g. an account of how a piece of medical equipment works, together with a request for money to buy one)

Describe some damage for a house insurance claim.

For the school newsletter, write an appeal for volunteers to join the school fundraising group.

Sample activities

- In pairs, read a letter to the editor in a local or national newspaper. Share ideas and make notes on points for a reply in support or disagreement. Each draft a reply. Compare content and structure and adjust their own draft if necessary.

- Using a context from their own experience, plan and draft an A4 news-sheet (e.g. to a playgroup parents' group, local political party, staff social club). Discuss the content, level of detail, the best way to organise the contents in the space available. Make a first draft on paper or screen; try out on other learners.

- Plan and draft a poem or short story for their own pleasure or as the basis for a contribution to an adult learners' anthology.

- In the context of researching and organising a group debate/formal discussion, plan, draft and write a speech to present to the group.

- In a group, use case studies with supporting material as necessary, to discuss, make decisions, and write notes on the length and level of detail required in different pieces of writing. Each person then writes one text in full. Circulate all texts round the group and edit as necessary to get right length and level of detail, e.g.: a letter to an official body in reply to one from them (to a bank about an overdraft/to the Benefits Agency about a claim); the text of a presentation to a group of enthusiasts on a topic of interest; a light-hearted account of a 'week in the life of an adult learner' for a centre magazine; a column along the lines of the *Guardian's* 'Pass Notes' on a famous person; an entry for a local guide book on an interesting walk.

- After reading about and discussing a local issue, write a short speech to be read out as part of a 'mini-debate' on the subject (e.g. whether a local school should close, whether a supermarket chain should be given planning permission to build in the neighbourhood).

- Think up ideas for a pie-in-the-sky proposition (e.g. Live Premier League football should return to terrestrial TV; the *Sun* should abolish 'Page 3'; all teenagers should tidy up after themselves). In a pair, plan and draft a defence of the proposition, structuring and organising points with supporting evidence, linking points appropriately, to convince the parties involved of the logic of the argument.

Using a word processor

The whole writing process

The word processor is potentially a useful tool to help learner writers, and there is evidence that it can be a strong motivator. It can be used for the whole writing process – planning, drafting, composing, editing and proof-reading – not merely as a typewriter for copying out a final neat version.

Word-processing skills

To make effective use of a word processor as part of a literacy programme, learners need some basic word-processing skills; otherwise, it can be simply another source of frustration. The most limiting factor is usually unfamiliarity with a keyboard. This has to be overcome to use a word processor for composition and hence for entering text. On the other hand, learners can become familiar with basic word-processing facilities by using a mouse on text provided, at a level suitable for their reading skills.

Teaching and learning intentions

Learning how to insert and delete letters and words, use the shift key for capitals, highlight, cut and paste, copy, drag and drop can give people a sense of the word processor's power and an idea of how they might use it in their own writing. These facilities can lead to a word processor being used simply as a form of electronic worksheet. It is important, as with any classroom activity, but especially when IT is involved, to be absolutely clear about the teaching and learning intentions when asking learners to use a word processor. It is easy to confuse developing word-processing skills with developing literacy skills.

See also in the key skills: Communication key skills level 2
Part A: In writing documents . . .
Part B: C2.3

At this level, adults can

write to communicate
information, ideas and opinions clearly and effectively, using length, format and style appropriate to purpose, content and audience

in a wide range of documents

 Writing composition

Wt/L2

Skills, knowledge and understanding

Adults should be taught to:

4 **use format and structure to organise writing for different purposes**

– understand which format, structure and layout are best for which sort of task, e.g. a table to organise information for reference or comparison, numbered points to separate stages in a process, paragraphs to develop an argument

– understand that some forms of writing follow standard formats and structures, e.g. memos, business letters, agendas and minutes of meetings

Example

Write a letter to an organisation using the format, structure and layout of a business letter.

5 **use formal and informal language appropriate to purpose and audience**

– understand that formality of language is a continuum, from informal speech with friends and family through to formal official written language

– know how to judge the appropriate level of formality suitable for different types of writing tasks and contexts, e.g. a letter to a friend, a safety report for work

Write a letter of condolence to a colleague.

6 **use different styles of writing for different purposes (e.g. persuasive techniques, supporting evidence, technical vocabulary)**

– understand that the style of writing involves choice of vocabulary, sentence length and structure, how the text is organised

– understand that what is appropriate style depends on purpose, audience, context

Write a notice for an important meeting (e.g. of a union, a parents' association/ tenants' association meeting), giving its purpose and explaining why people should attend.

Sample activities

- Devise and structure a simple questionnaire on a word processor, for a mini-survey (e.g. the proportions of the week adult learners spend watching TV, playing sport, doing a hobby, doing voluntary work, reading for pleasure, studying). Present the results in a table to show the most popular activities and to draw comparisons, e.g. between men and women, different age groups. Use the information as a stimulus for discussion.

- Practise setting out and drafting formal letters in different contexts (e.g. a letter of enquiry, complaint, thanking a company for good service).

- Discuss levels of formality, then write about the same topic for different audiences: e.g. two letters about noise disturbance in the neighbourhood, one to a former neighbour who has moved away, and the other to the local council.

- Look at formal and informal ways of wording invitations (e.g. from a wedding magazine). Draft invitations to various events (e.g. an eighteenth-birthday party, a silver wedding, a retirement presentation, a reception at the mayor's parlour), choosing appropriate language and style.

- Working in a pair or group, investigate a topic which provokes strong feelings (e.g. hunting with hounds). Make notes under the headings of known facts, supporting evidence, opinions. Use these as the basis for one person writing in favour and one against. Compare persuasive styles, e.g. the way evidence is used, emotive language, use of stylistic devices such as rhetorical questions, exaggeration, direct appeals to the reader.

- Compare some technical and non-technical writing (e.g. the weather forecast in a daily paper, the shipping forecast); then identify their own 'expert' subject. Draft the openings to two different texts in the same subject area – one for a general audience and one for a more specialist audience – choosing the type of text, title, vocabulary, level of detail, layout, for the different readers (e.g. *The Pleasures of Cake Decoration* and *Advanced Cake Decoration Techniques*; *Simple Car Maintenance* and *How to Strip an Engine*).

- Use the world-wide web to visit sites that will explain technical vocabulary associated with different occupations, or, for example, children's diseases or disorders. Copy and paste the explanations from the web site into a Word document.

Using a word processor *(continued)*

Literacy benefits?

When will working on screen provide an additional *literacy* benefit? When will it make it easier to practise a particular leaning point, say the use of capital letters? When will it be doing what can be done as effectively on paper but with an additional motivational factor? When might it be inappropriate? When will it provide a genuine extension to a task, such as: building up a personal dictionary in a table, allowing new words to be slotted in in alphabetical order; planning, drafting, composing and editing a piece of writing over time; preparing a document where layout and formatting are important; composing and sending an e-mail message? These sorts of question enable the teacher to be clear about the benefits to the learner and to judge when these will outweigh any drawbacks, such as getting access to machines, or learners' slowness on the keyboard.

Spell checkers

Spell-checking facilities can be a great boon, but need to be introduced at the right time, when the learner can:

- spell well enough for the alternative suggestions to be of use;
- read well enough to evaluate which suggestion is the right one.

Practising composition

For unconfident writers the greatest advantage of becoming proficient on a word processor is often seen as the ability to produce mistake-free text, but the word processor does not guarantee this. Neatly produced writing can still fail to make sense, or be inappropriate for its purpose. These depend on the writer's ability to handle the mechanics of sentence composition, vocabulary selection, textual organisation, etc. Using the word processor to practise writing different types of text from scratch can help learners experiment with word order, choice of language, paragraph development in a less laborious way than on paper. As they become more proficient with the word processor, so they can exploit its facilities to help their composition, which should feed into their literacy development.

See also in the key skills:

Communication key skills level 2
Part A: In writing documents . . .
Part B: C2.3

 *At this level, adults can*

write to communicate
information, ideas and opinions clearly and effectively, using length, format and style appropriate to purpose, content and audience

in a wide range of documents

Text Focus **Writing composition** **Wt/L2**

Skills, knowledge and understanding

Adults should be taught to:

7 proof-read and revise writing for accuracy and meaning

– understand that, as well as checking for errors of spelling, grammar and general sense, proof-reading enables the writer to spot: unintended ambiguity (where meaning can be taken in more than one way); long-windedness or repetition (where the same point could be made more concisely); compression (where too many points are pushed into too few words and the sense is muddled)

– understand that revising these might involve rewriting some sentences as well as adding or removing individual words

Example

Plan, draft, proof-read and revise an assignment so that the meaning is clearly expressed and the spelling and grammar are accurate.

Sentence Focus **Grammar and punctuation** **Ws/L2**

Skills, knowledge and understanding

Adults should be taught to:

1 construct complex sentences

– understand that complex sentences have more variety of structure than simple and compound sentences, and that this stops the writing becoming boring

– understand that complex sentences always have more than one part (clause) and the parts are more closely related to each other than two separate sentences

– understand that simple or compound sentences are preferable for some types of writing, e.g. instructions or directions

– understand that effective writing often uses a mixture of simple, compound and complex sentences

Example

Write a letter or report using complex sentences effectively.

2 use correct grammar (e.g. subject–verb agreement, correct and consistent use of tense)

– understand that, in complex sentences which may have several parts, particular care is needed to check subject–verb agreement

– understand that the choice of tense depends on the task

– understand that in longer texts the writer needs to keep checking back while writing, not at the end, and to check that the tense remains consistent

– understand that, when writing texts such as impersonal reports, passive verb forms are useful to keep the focus on the action rather than on who performs it, e.g. *It has recently been revealed that the association is losing money.*

Write a formal report, in the context of paid or voluntary work, which sustains consistent tense and subject–verb agreement.

Sample activities

- Practise proof-reading their own work for different purposes: scanning each line for spellings that 'don't look right'; reading 'aloud' (this can be under their breath in a whisper, but the important thing is to listen as well as look) to spot grammatical errors, missing or repeated words, and where meaning could be expressed more clearly or concisely. Amend, revise and re-read.

- Exchange their writing with a partner at proof-reading stage; each act as sub-editor for the other, pointing out any places where the sense needs to be clarified for the reader.

Sample activities

- Increase their awareness of the range of complex sentence patterns by experimenting in a pair with what can be done with them, e.g.: using cards or on screen, try moving words around to see what can go where and still make grammatical sense; delete/cover with post-it strips which words can be omitted, and identify which are essential for sense; try expanding, contracting and combining sentences; highlight in the same colour words that relate to each other (e.g. nouns with their adjectives, verbs with their adverbs).

- In pairs or in a group, each person takes the same set of six or eight simple and compound sentences on an item of local news. Rewrite them as two or three sentences to fill a 'news in brief' slot, changing the word order, adding/deleting words, using a linking word from a list if necessary, but keeping the overall sense and details of the original. Compare the old and new versions.

- Use 'highlight', 'drag and drop' to move the text in complex sentences around, so that the meaning is clear. Insert punctuation where necessary.

- Read two or three paragraphs from a newspaper article; highlight verbs, using a different colour for a different tense. Discuss findings and note how, even when an account is written mainly in the past tense, there may be verbs in the present and the future as well (e.g. to indicate an on-going situation, a future happening). Choose a suitable subject and draft two or three paragraphs in the style of the article, paying particular attention to tenses. Read and analyse the use of tenses in their own writing.

- Raise their awareness of the difference between active and passive verbs by transforming active verbs in given sentences into passives, and discussing what happens.

See also in the key skills: Communication key skills level 2
Part A: In writing documents . . .
Part B: C2.3

LEVEL 2 *At this level, adults can*

write to communicate
information, ideas and opinions clearly and effectively, using length, format and style appropriate to purpose, content and audience

in a wide range of documents

Sentence Focus   **Grammar and punctuation**   **Ws/L2**

Skills, knowledge and understanding

Adults should be taught to:

3 use pronouns so that their meaning is clear

– understand that pronouns are used to refer to nouns, to avoid having to repeat the noun each time

– know that, when using pronouns, it must be clear to what or to whom they refer, and to check this when proof-reading

– know the term *pronoun* and be able to identify personal pronouns: *I, me, we, us, you, they, them*

– understand how these link to the concept of first, second and third person, singular and plural, and subject–verb agreement

4 punctuate sentences correctly, and use punctuation accurately (e.g. commas, apostrophes, inverted commas)

– understand when commas are needed in sentences (e.g. to separate items in a list and parts of some complex sentences, to enclose extra information), and that commas should not be used in place of full stops

– understand the use of the apostrophe to show a missing letter(s) (e.g. *they're, we've, I'm*)

– know the full verb equivalents and that the writer can choose short or full forms depending on the formality required

– understand the difference between *it's* (*it is*) and *its (belonging to it*)

– understand the use of the apostrophe to show where a final *–s* indicates that something belongs to someone/thing

– understand the use of inverted commas for direct speech and to indicate a quotation

Example

Recount an experience or incident, e.g. as part of a letter of complaint, using pronouns with clarity.

Write a short story or account of an experience (e.g. for an adult learners' anthology, a community magazine), using a range of punctuation accurately to support meaning.

Sample activities

- Increase their awareness of possible pronoun ambiguity by reading a story or an account of an experience written by a young child where it is not always clear who or what the pronouns are referring to. Annotate the text with a reader's questions about its possible meaning. Amend the text to make the meaning clear. Write down some advice to give the child about using pronouns.

- Read a copy of a newspaper article in which some of the nouns and pronouns have been removed in the last paragraph. Re-write this paragraph with appropriate nouns and pronouns, deciding where pronouns could be used and where a noun would be necessary to make the meaning clear. In a pair, identify some guidelines for avoiding ambiguous pronouns in this type of writing.

- Use 'Find and Replace' to substitute pronouns *(my, her, his, our, their)* for nouns.

- Reinforce and extend their knowledge and use of punctuation by writing a 'Punctuation serial': the teacher writes the first paragraph of a story without any punctuation (based on two or three characters likely to appeal to/amuse learners); they punctuate the paragraph for homework, discuss it in the next class and suggest developments for Episode 2; the teacher writes the paragraph up, and learners punctuate it, and so on. The teacher brings in more demanding punctuation and more complex sentence structures through the episodes.

- Establish punctuation routines in their own writing, e.g.: place a post-it on the page/screen as a reminder; always stop at the end of a paragraph/section and re-read for sense and punctuation; read aloud to someone at home to spot omissions; exchange work with another learner and do a 'punctuation check' for each other; identify their own 'punctuation black spots' to work on (e.g. check every *its/it's* – could it be replaced with *it is*? If so, it needs an apostrophe).

Inverted commas, semi-colons, colons, dashes

Inverted commas largely relate to narrative writing or to quotations, so can be practised in very specific contexts. Setting out direct speech is often more of a challenge to learners than use of the speech marks themselves. Semi-colons, colons and dashes can often be exemplified in texts such as leaflets or brochures where single points are listed or bulleted from a common stem. The semi-colon as a way of separating two complete short 'sentences' that are nonetheless closely related can help some learners to break the habit of wrongly using commas in this context.

Apostrophes without tears?

Apostrophes relate closely to grammatical structure. The **omissive** apostrophe signals a missing letter in contracted forms of words or phrases associated with spoken language and informal writing, especially in direct speech in narrative. Adults are more likely to 'see the point' of them if they learn them in the context of less formal versions of full-form, more formal equivalents. They also usefully fall into certain main 'families': negative verb forms (e.g. *can't/cannot, haven't/have not, shouldn't/should not*, etc.) and pronoun + verb combinations (e.g. *I'm/I am, you're/you are*, etc.).

Possessive apostrophes appear to baffle most of the country and produce plenty of column inches per year in favour of their retention or abandonment. The easiest form to teach is probably the –'s for singular possessives: *Fred's feet, The Shakespeare's Head Hotel; This bloke's wife is my sister*. If the words can be re-framed as *the something of something (feet of Fred*, etc.) then a possessive apostrophe is needed. If adults are also taught explicitly about pluralisation and the role of –s/–es in making nouns plural, they should have a reasonable chance of distinguishing the singular –'s possessive from the plural –s.

The whole picture gets cloudier for many people when introduced to the plural possessive –s' form and to possessive pronouns, which (apparently inconsistently) use an –s without an apostrophe *(yours, hers, its, ours, theirs)*. Sorting *its* and *it's* **should** be simple enough: forget the possessive angle altogether – if *its* can be substituted with *it is* then it's *it's!*

See also in the key skills:

Communication key skills level 2
Part A: In writing documents . . .
Part B: C2.3

*At this level,
adults can*

write to communicate
information, ideas and opinions
clearly and effectively, using
length, format and style
appropriate to purpose, content
and audience

in a wide range of documents

Word Focus   **Spelling and handwriting**   **Ww/L2**

Skills, knowledge and understanding

Adults should be taught to:

1 spell correctly words used most often
in work, studies and daily life,
including familiar technical words

– know and apply a range of methods (visual,
phonetic, kinaesthetic, use of analogies and
mnemonics) to help learn and remember
correct spellings

– understand how knowledge of word roots,
prefixes and suffixes can support spelling,
including the spelling of technical words

– understand that some polysyllabic words
have unstressed vowel sounds, and that it
is often helpful to segment the word into
its parts, e.g. *diff-er-ent, inter-est-ing,
poison-ous*

Example

Be confident enough to choose the most
precise words for the task in their own
writing, not necessarily the easiest words to
spell, by applying strategies to attempt and
check their spelling and by knowing when to
double-check with an outside source.

2 produce legible text

Handwrite legibly and with minimum
alterations a piece of writing to be read by
someone they do not know personally, e.g. a
letter to the council or tax office.

Use a word processor to prepare a text for
circulation to more than one person, e.g. a
report of parents' fundraising success to go to
the school governors.

Sample activities

- In a pair or group, share some mnemonics to remember tricky spellings and write them in their own spelling dictionary, e.g. *'necessary' has a collar and a pair of socks; 'rhythm' has your two hands moving; e+a + a+e = separate.*

- In pairs, identify and write down the root word from a list of words ending in *–ly* (e.g. *lovely, love; finally, final; actually, actual; practically, practical; differently, different; immediately, immediate; sincerely, sincere).* From the evidence, formulate a rule for adding *–ly* and test it out on another list of words.

Spelling and word structure

- Use and spell possessive pronouns correctly, e.g. *their, theirs; your, yours; my, mine.*

- Understand and spell prefixes such as *auto–, bi–, trans–, tele–, circum–.*

- Read and spell the suffix *–cian.*

- Distinguish between the spelling and meaning of homophones such as: *ate, eight; grate, great; rain, reign, rein.*

- Spell unstressed vowels in polysyllabic words, e.g. *interest, different.*

- Identify 'problem words' (e.g. *immediately, discussion, remember, interesting, argument, occasionally)* or groups of words (e.g. *tough, through, thorough, enough).* Make a set of memo cards by writing the individual word in large print on a postcard, highlighting the tricky parts, with an example of the word used correctly in a sentence underneath. Keep the cards in pocket and look through them whenever there's a spare moment; make a new set when those are learnt.

- Write out a piece of their own work carefully by hand for a display of learners' writing for an end-of-year/Adult Learners' Week celebration.

- Word process a piece of their own work to contribute to a magazine of writing by adult learners to be available in a local job centre/community centre/library.

Glossary

active and passive	many verbs can be active or passive. For example, *bite: The dog bit Ben* (active); *Ben was bitten by the dog* (passive). In the active sentence, the subject *(the dog)* performs the action. In the passive sentence, the subject *(Ben)* is on the receiving end of the action.
	In a passive sentence, the 'doer' (or agent) may be identified using *by: Ben was bitten by the dog*. But very often, in passive sentences, the agent is unknown or insignificant, and therefore not identified: *The computer has been repaired*. Passive forms are common in impersonal, formal styles, for example: *Application forms may be obtained from the address below*.
adjective	a word that describes somebody or something. Adjectives either come before a noun (e.g. *a busy day*), or after 'linking' verbs such as *be, get, seem, look* (e.g. *I'm busy*).
adverb	a word that gives extra meaning to a verb, an adjective, another adverb or a whole sentence, e.g.: *I really enjoyed the party; She's really nice; He works really slowly; Really, he should do better*. Many adverbs are formed by adding *–ly* to an adjective, for example *quickly, dangerously, nicely*, but there are many adverbs that do not end in *–ly*. However, some *–ly* words are adjectives, not adverbs (e.g. *lovely, silly, friendly*).
	In many cases, adverbs tell us how (manner), where (place) when (time) or how often (frequency) something happens. Other adverbs show degree of intensity *(very slowly)*, the attitude of the speaker to what he or she is saying *(perhaps, obviously)*, or connections in meaning between sentences *(however, finally)*.
adverbial phrase	a group of words that functions in the same way as a single adverb, e.g. *by car, to work, last week, three times a day, first of all, of course*.
agreement (or concord)	in some cases the form of a verb changes according to its subject, so the verb and subject 'agree', e.g. *I am/he is/they are; I was/you were; I like/she likes, I don't/he doesn't*.
alliteration	when two or more adjacent words, or words near each other, begin with the same sound (**phoneme**), e.g. *Flora's Flower Shop, the Luton Locarno*.
ambiguity	a word, phrase or statement that has more than one possible interpretation, sometimes arising from unclear grammatical relationships (e.g. *Police shot man with knife*). Ambiguity may be accidental or deliberate, and is often a source of humour. In poetry it often serves to extend the meaning beyond the literal.
analogy	the perception of similarity between two things; relating something known to something new. In spelling, using known spellings to spell unknown words (e.g. *night–knight–right–sight–light–fright*). In reading, using knowledge of words to attempt previously unseen words.
antonym	a word with a meaning opposite to another (e.g. *hot–cold, satisfaction–dissatisfaction*).
appropriate	describes a text, word, utterance or style that is suitably phrased for its intended audience and form. 'Appropriate' accepts that different contexts require different treatments and is in this respect to be differentiated from 'correct', which is more concerned with the right grammatical formulation of an expression.
articulation	the production of different speech sounds through the use of the speech organs: pharynx, tongue, lips, jaw, soft and hard palate.
audience	the people addressed by a text. The term includes listeners, readers of print, film/TV audiences, and users of information technology.
blend	the process of combining phonemes into larger elements such as clusters, syllables and words. Also refers to a combination of two or more phonemes, particularly at the beginning and end of words, e.g. *st, str, nt, pl, nd*.
chronological	an adjective that describes writing organised in terms of sequences of events.
clause	a structural unit, smaller than a sentence but larger than a phrase or word, which contains a verb. A **main clause** makes sense on its own and can form a complete sentence *(It was raining.)* A **subordinate** (sometimes called dependent) **clause** amplifies the main clause, but does not make complete sense on its own and cannot stand as an independent grammatical unit *(when we went out)*. When attached to a main clause, a subordinate clause makes a complete sentence, e.g. *It was raining when we went out. /When we went out it was raining*. Subordinate clauses can sometimes be abbreviated to phrases, omitting verb and subject, which are understood from the context, e.g. *When in Rome, do as the Romans do*.

cloze	an exercise in which certain words are deleted from a text and a gap left. The learner's task is to supply the missing words. Words can be deleted in a specific way (e.g. adjectives, conjunctions), or randomly (every *n*th word).
coherence	the underlying logical connectedness of a text, whereby concepts and relationships are relevant to each other and it is possible to make plausible inferences about underlying meaning.
comma splicing	use of a comma where a full stop is required, thus 'splicing' together two sentences that should be separate.
common	used of words, patterns of spelling and grammatical constructions that occur frequently.
comparative and superlative	forms of adjectives that convey different degrees of intensity. The comparative expresses a relationship of degree between two: *taller, happier, more secluded;* the superlative expresses the limits of the quality: *tallest, happiest, most secluded.* Some adjectives use the endings *–er/–est;* others, usually longer adjectives, use *more/most.* The 'rule' is that only one of these methods should be used at once. Comparative and superlative forms follow certain spelling patterns when the endings are added, e.g. *healthy/healthier/healthiest; sad, sadder, saddest.*
complex information	materials containing complex information present a number of ideas, some of which may be abstract, detailed or require learners to deal with sensitive issues. In such material, the relationship of ideas and the lines of reasoning may not be immediately clear, and specialised vocabulary and complicated sentence structures may be used.
compound word	a word made up of two other words: *football, headrest, playground.*
comprehension	the level of understanding of a written text or spoken utterance. With **literal comprehension**, the reader has access to the surface details of the text, and can recall details that have been directly related. With **inferential comprehension**, the reader can read meanings that are not directly explained. For example, the reader would be able to make inferences about the time of year from information given about temperature, weather, etc. and from characters' behaviour and dialogue. With **evaluative comprehension**, the reader can offer an opinion on the effectiveness of the text for its purpose.
conjunction	a word used to link clauses within a sentence, a type of **connective**. **Co-ordinating conjunctions** (e.g. *and, but, or, so*) join two clauses of equal weight into a compound sentence; **subordinating conjunctions** (e.g. *when, while, before, after, since, until, if, because, although, that*) introduce a subordinate clause in a complex sentence.
connective	a word or phrase that links different parts of a text (clauses, sentences, paragraphs). Connectives can be conjunctions (e.g. *but, when, because*) or connecting adverbs (e.g. *however, then, therefore*). Connectives maintain the cohesion of a text, e.g. by: addition *(and, also, furthermore);* opposition *(however, but, nevertheless, on the other hand);* cause *(because, this means, therefore);* time *(just then, immediately, as soon as possible).* Particular connectives tend to occur in particular text types, e.g.: of time, in chronological narratives; of opposition or cause, when presenting an argument or persuading to a viewpoint. Pronouns (e.g. *A survey of adult learners will take place shortly. It will be the largest of its kind to date.)* and prepositional phrases (e.g. *in other words, after all that*) can also act as connectives.
consonant	a speech sound that obstructs the flow of air through the vocal tract; for example, the flow of air is obstructed by the lips in *p* and by the tongue in *l.* The term also refers to those letters of the alphabet whose typical value is to represent such sounds, namely all except *a, e, i, o, u.* The letter *y* can represent a consonant sound *(yes)* or a vowel sound *(happy).*
context	the non-linguistic situation in which spoken or written language is used.
decode	to translate the visual code of the letters into a word.
descriptive	defines text that attempts to describe an event, a process or a state without passing judgement on it, or offering an explanation of it. Because of its concern to convey an experience as accurately as possible, descriptive text often makes greater use of adjectives and figurative language than other forms of writing.
detailed reading	indicates a form of reading that is at the opposite end of the spectrum from skimming or scanning. Detailed reading involves careful reading in order to extract specific information, but also to gain a complete understanding of the text's intentions and the way in which language choice and syntax combine to produce a particular message.
digraph	two letters representing one phoneme: *bath; train; ch/ur/ch.*
Dolch list	(see high frequency words.)
etymology	the study of the origin and history of words.

everyday	an adjective used to describe text, language and situations that are the daily experience of most people.
explanatory	an adjective used to describe text written to explain how or why something happens. Explanatory text tends to use connectives expressing cause and effect (e.g. *so, therefore, as a result*) and time (e.g. *later, meanwhile*) and the passive voice (e.g. *Tax is usually deducted at source*) more than many other forms of text.
explicit/implicit knowledge	native speakers of a language know implicitly how their language works through using it. Being specifically taught about aspects of form, structure and usage makes implicit knowledge explicit, enabling learners to consciously think and talk about how the language works, and how they use it themselves.
familiar	describes contexts, situations, sources, topics or words of which the learner has some prior knowledge or experience.
feedback	the on-going reaction speakers receive from their listeners which helps them evaluate the success of their communication. Feedback may be verbal or non-verbal (e.g. facial expressions, gestures).
formal	depicts a style of language where the choice of words, syntax and address is determined by a distance from the audience, which may be dictated by the context (e.g. a letter of application, official documents) or the result of a lack of knowledge of this audience. Formal language tends to be characterised by more elaborate grammatical structures and by longer and more conservative vocabulary (e.g. *receive* rather than *get*, *gratuity* rather than *tip*).
format	the way in which a text is arranged or presented (e.g. as a book, leaflet, essay, video, audiotape) or the way in which it is structured (e.g. the use made of headings, sub-headings, diagrams/photographs with captions).
genre	originally an identifiable category or type of literary composition (e.g. novel, drama, short story, poetry, autobiography). Now used more widely to refer to different types of written form, literary and non-literary (e.g. story, list, letter). Different genres have recognisable features of language and structure.
gist	the main point or idea of a text. Reading for gist is thus reading for identification of the main point only.
grammar	the conventions that govern the relationships between words in any language, including the study of word order and changes in words. Study of grammar enhances both reading and writing skills and supports effective communication.
grapheme	written representation of a sound; may consist of one or more letters; for example, the phoneme *s* can be represented by the graphemes *s, se, c, sc* and *ce* as in <u>s</u>un, mou<u>se</u>, <u>c</u>ity, <u>s</u>cien<u>ce</u>.
graphic knowledge	the ability to understand the key features of the English writing system, including the basic shape of the letters, the plural form of nouns, spelling patterns in verb endings, the difference between upper and lower case, etc. At its more complicated, this term may also be used to show understanding of the other features of a text, typographical or visual, that hold a clue to its meaning.
high frequency words	words that occur frequently; someone who is unable to recognise or use these words will therefore be at a disadvantage. A number of attempts have been made (notably by Dolch) to identify those words that learners most need to acquire in order to advance in their learning.
homonym	words that have the same spelling or pronunciation as another, but a different meaning or origin.
homophone	words that have the same sound as another but a different meaning or different spelling: *read/reed; pair/pear; right/write/rite*.
hypertext	a word coined in 1965 to describe electronic texts, where a collection of documents contain cross-references or 'links' that allow the reader to move easily from one document to another with the aid of a browser program.
ICT	Information and Communication Technology.
imperative	a form of the verb that expresses a command or instruction (e.g. *Hold this! Take the second left*).
informal	depicts a style of language where choices of words, grammatical construction and address are determined by a connection with the audience which may be actual or sought. Informal language tends to be more colloquial and familiar than formal language, to use less technical or complex vocabulary and to have simple grammatical structures.
instructional	describes text written to help readers achieve certain goals (such texts include recipes, vehicle repair manuals, self-assembly instructions). Instructional text tends to use imperative verbs often placed at the beginning of sentences to form a series of commands, and time-related connectives.

intonation	the way in which changes in the musical pitch of the voice are used to structure speech and to contribute to meaning. Among other functions, intonation may distinguish questions from statements (as in *Sure? Sure!*), or indicate contrastive and emotive stress (as in *I said <u>two</u>, not three,* or *I just <u>hate</u> that advertisement!*).
key words	the words that carry the substance of a phrase or the meaning of a sentence. Identifying the key words of a text is therefore a means of understanding its gist. The term is also applied to those words in any subject that, it is considered, learners have to understand if they are to progress.
kinaesthetic	related to voluntary bodily movement. Some learners find that tracing patterns of words with their finger on the page, or 'drawing' them in the air, helps to secure spelling patterns in the memory.
language experience	an approach to learning that uses the learner's own words to provide the basis for language work. Typically, a teacher adopting a language experience approach will produce a written version of a 'spoken text' supplied by the learner, so that there is a written text with which the learner is familiar, to be used for further work in reading and writing.
letter string	a group of letters that together represent a **phoneme** or **morpheme**.
limited, meaningful vocabulary	a person with a limited meaningful vocabulary is able to recognise and use a restricted number of words only, but these words are important for that person to function effectively in their everyday and working lives.
lower case	a term used to describe small letters, that is all letters that are not capital letters. In print, lower-case letters will be of varying size, with some having 'ascenders' and some having 'descenders' (parts of the letter rising above and below the main body of the letter, respectively), and some having neither.
medium	the way in which language is transmitted from one person, or an agency, to another. The three basic media of language are phonic (speech), graphic (writing) and signing (sign language for hearing impaired people). The term is also used to denote the means of communication (e.g. television, telephone, film, radio, computer, press).
metalanguage	the language we use when talking about language itself. It includes words like *sentence, noun, paragraph, preposition*. Those who understand these concepts are able to talk about language quite precisely; thus, acquisition of metalanguage is seen as a crucial step in developing awareness of and proficiency in communication, particularly in written language.
metaphor	a figurative expression where something is written or spoken of in terms usually associated with something else. In literary composition, metaphor can give imaginative force to expression, e.g. Romeo to the supposedly dead Juliet: *Beauty's ensign yet / Is crimson in thy lips and in thy cheeks, / And death's pale flag is not advancèd there.* Much everyday language uses metaphor (e.g. to *launch* a new book/film); overworked metaphors can soon become tired and clichéd (e.g. *at the end of the day*).
mnemonic	a device to aid memory, for instance to learn particular spelling patterns or spellings: *<u>I</u> <u>G</u>o <u>H</u>ome <u>T</u>onight; There is <u>a</u> <u>rat</u> in sepa<u>rat</u>e.*
mind map	a way of writing ideas as they arise, without organising them into the form of a written text. It is used in teaching writing to enable learners to feel clear about what they want to write, before thinking about how to write it. A similar technique is a spidergraph.
morpheme	the smallest unit of meaning. A word may consist of one morpheme *(house)*, two morphemes *(house/s; hous/ing)* or three or more morphemes *(house/keep/ing; un/happi/ness)*. **Suffixes** and **prefixes** are morphemes.
narrative	describes text that re-tells events, often in chronological sequence. Narrative text may be purely fictional, or it may include some information; it may be in prose or poetic form.
noun	a word that denotes somebody or something (e.g. *My younger <u>sister</u> won some <u>money</u> in a <u>competition</u>.*). **Countable** nouns can be singular (only one) or plural (more than one), e.g. *sister/sisters, problem/problems, party/parties*. **Mass** nouns do not normally occur in the plural (e.g. *butter, cotton, electricity, money, happiness*).
	Nouns that make non-specific reference to things, people, creatures, etc. are called **common** nouns, e.g. *sister, money, competition, dog*.
	Those that name a concept or idea are called **abstract** nouns, e.g. *happiness, love, justice, grief*.
	A **collective** noun refers to a group (e.g. *crowd, flock, team*). Although these are singular in form, we often think of them as plural in meaning and use them with a plural verb. For example, if we say *The team <u>have</u> won all <u>their</u> games so far* we think of *the team* as *they* (rather than *it*).
	Proper nouns are the names of specific people, places, organisations, etc. These normally begin with a capital letter (e.g. *Amanda, Birmingham, Microsoft, Islam, November*).

organisational features (of text)	refers to those aspects of the visual display of text that give a clue to its status and to its relation to other pieces of text. Such features include: contents pages, chapter headings and other sub-headings, bullet-point lists, captions to photographs and illustrations, text presented in special display boxes, tables, footnotes, indexes, etc.
paragraph	a section of a piece of writing. A new paragraph marks a change of focus, a change of time, a change of place or a change of speaker in a passage or dialogue. A new paragraph begins on a new line, usually with a one-line gap separating it from the previous paragraph, and sometimes indented. Paragraphing helps writers to organise their thoughts, and helps readers to follow the storyline, argument or dialogue.
passive	(See **active and passive**.)
person	a grammatical term referring to the use of pronouns and verbs to indicate: direct reference to the speaker – first person *(I said..., I am...)*; to the addressee – second person *(you said..., you are...)*; or to others – the third person *(she said...they are...)*.
personal keywords	refers to those words that are important to learners in terms of their daily lives; no two people's personal keywords will be exactly the same, since they will include, for example, a person's address, the names of family members, employer's name and address, etc.
persuasive	describes a text that aims to persuade the reader. A continuous persuasive text typically consists of a statement of the viewpoint, arguments and evidence for this thesis, possibly some arguments and evidence supporting a different view, and a final summary or recommendation. Other types of persuasive text (e.g. advertisements) use a combination of textual features including words, sounds and images, and intertextual knowledge in order to persuade.
phoneme	the smallest contrastive unit of sound in a word. There are approximately 44 phonemes in English (the number varies depending on the accent). A phoneme may have variant pronunciations in different positions; for example, the first and last sounds in the word 'little' are variants of the phoneme /l/. A phoneme may be represented by one, two, three or four letters. The following words end in the same phoneme (with the corresponding letters underlined): *to, shoe, through*.
phonic	relating to vocal, or speech, sounds. As a plural noun, **phonics** denotes a method of teaching reading and spelling that is based on establishing the link between the sound of a word and its graphical representation.
phonological awareness	awareness of sounds within words, demonstrated, for example, by the ability to segment and blend component sounds and to recognise and generate sound patterns such as rhyme.
phrase	a group of two or more words smaller than a clause, forming a grammatical unit. Phrases can be structured around a noun *(her new red dress)*, a verb *(has been talking, will be coming)*, an adverb *(I will be home as soon as possible)*, an adjective *(That house is larger than mine.)*, a preposition *(I saw a man in a raincoat.)*.
pitch	the auditory sense that a sound is 'higher' or 'lower'.
plural	form of a noun, pronoun or verb that indicates there are more than one. In English, plural nouns are usually formed by inflection, adding *–s* or *–es*. Plural nouns and pronouns generally need their partner verbs to be plural. (See **agreement**.)
prefix	a **morpheme** that can be added to the beginning of a word to change its meaning, e.g. *inedible, disappear, supermarket, unintentional*.
preposition	a word, like *at, over, by* and *with*, that is usually followed by a noun phrase. Prepositions often indicate time *(at midnight/during the film/on Friday)*, position *(at the station/in a field)* or direction *(to the station/over a fence)*. There are many other meanings, including possession *(of this street)*, means *(by car)* and accompaniment *(with me)*.
pronoun	is a word that stands in for a noun or noun phrase. There are several kinds of pronoun: personal pronouns *(I/me, you, he/him, she/her, we/us, they/them, it)*, possessive pronouns *(mine, yours, his, hers, ours, theirs, its)*, reflexive pronouns *(myself, herself, themselves)*, indefinite pronouns *(someone, anything, nobody, everything)*, interrogative pronouns *(who/whom, whose, which, what)* and relative pronouns *(who/whom, whose, which, that)*.
proof-read	to check a piece of work thoroughly before final publication.
punctuation	a way of marking text to help readers' understanding. The most commonly used marks in English are: apostrophe, colon, comma, dash, ellipsis, exclamation mark, full stop, hyphen, semi-colon and speech marks (inverted commas).

register	a variety of language selected for use in a specific social situation. In particular, the register differentiates formal from informal use of language.
regular	an adjective used to describe words, typically verbs and nouns, that conform to general rules. It is possible to predict the plural form of a regular noun, or the simple past and past participle form of a regular verb; it is not possible to do so with irregular nouns and verbs.
repeated language patterns	a phrase to describe the repetition of vocabulary and the recurrence of structural features in grammar and spelling that enables a learner to make accurate predictions about the sound and the sense of words and constructions, and therefore obtain meaning from text.
root word	a word to which **prefixes** and **suffixes** may be added to make other words: for example in *unclear, clearly, cleared,* the root word is *clear.*
patterns	grammar and spelling that enable the learner to make accurate predictions about the sound and the sense of words and constructions, and thus obtain meaning from text.
scan	to look over a text very quickly, trying to find information by locating a key word.
segment	to break a word or part of a word down into its component **phonemes**, for example: *c-a-t; ch-a-t; ch-ar-t; g-r-ou-n-d; s-k-i-n.*
sentence	a sentence can be simple, compound or complex.

A **simple sentence** consists of one clause (e.g. *It was late*).

A **compound sentence** has two or more main clauses of equal weight joined by *and, or, but* or *so* (e.g. *It was late but I wasn't tired*).

A **complex sentence** consists of a main clause that includes one or more subordinate clauses (e.g. *Although it was late, I wasn't tired*).

In writing, sentences are marked by using a capital letter at the beginning, and a full stop (or question mark or exclamation mark) at the end.

As well as being described by structure, sentences can be classified by purpose. A statement is a sentence primarily designed to convey information *(I am happy.)*. A question seeks to obtain information (Are you happy?). A command or imperative instructs someone to do something *(Cheer up!)*. An exclamation conveys the speaker's/writer's reaction *(How happy you look today!)*.

short	denotes words, sentences and texts of such a length as to be accessible to learners and to enable them to experience a sense of achievement at having successfully decoded them. *Short* and *long* are terms also applied to vowel sounds.
sight vocabulary	words that a learner recognises on sight without having to decode them or work them out.
simile	a figurative expression where the writer creates an image in the reader's mind by explicitly comparing a subject to something else: *Threshed corn lay like grit of ivory / Or solid as cement in two-lugged sacks.* ('The Barn', Seamus Heaney). Similes are widely used in everyday language: *as happy as a lark, as strong as an ox.* Many are idiomatic: *he smokes like a chimney.*
simple	when applied to narrative, words, sentences, an adjective that indicates a basic, uncomplicated structure. A simple sentence structure, for example, follows the standard pattern of subject, verb and, optionally, object; a simple narrative will follow a chronological sequence and be told from one viewpoint only.
skim	to read to get an initial overview of the subject matter and main ideas of a passage.
standard English	the variety of English used in public communication, particularly in writing. It is not limited to a particular region and can be spoken with any accent. There are differences in vocabulary and grammar between standard English and other varieties: for example, *we were robbed* and *look at those trees* are standard English; *we was robbed* and *look at them trees* are non-standard. To communicate effectively in a range of situations – written and oral – it is necessary to be able to use standard English, and to recognise when it is appropriate to use it in preference to any other variety. Standard British English is not the only standard variety; other English-speaking countries, such as the United States and Australia, have their own standard forms.
straightforward	describes subjects and materials that learners often meet in their work, studies or other activities. Straightforward content is put across in a direct way with the main points easily identifiable; usually the sentence structures of such texts are simple, and learners will be familiar with the vocabulary.

structure	the way in which letters are built up into words, words built up into sentences and sentences built up into paragraphs, etc. Learners use structural features to process new words (e.g. by recognising that the suffix *–ly* usually indicates an adverb, or that the prefix *re–* will convey the sense of 'again'), new constructions (e.g. that initial speech marks are likely to indicate the start of something somebody said, that an exclamation mark denotes a rise in volume or emotion) and new forms of organisation (e.g. a new paragraph will introduce a new idea, a new time, or perhaps a new viewpoint).
style	a difficult term to define because of its many uses. The selection of a set of linguistic features from all the possibilities in a language; style can be defined in relation to context, purpose, audience, e.g. *formal* or *informal, non-specialist* or *technical*. Famous writers often demonstrate particular characteristics of style, making their work easily recognisable, e.g. *Shakespearean style*. All language users have the opportunity to make linguistic choices that will determine the style of a piece of writing or an utterance.
subject	a grammatical term for the agent in a sentence. The subject is the 'who' or 'what' that the sentence is about. The subject of a sentence must 'agree' with its verb: e.g. a singular subject requires a singular verb. When the verb is in the active voice, the subject of the sentence is the 'doer': e.g. *Dave met Lynette at the station*. When the verb is in the passive voice, the subject is the recipient of the action, e.g. *Lynette was met by Dave at the station*. (See **active and passive**.)
suffix	a **morpheme** that is added to the end of a word. There are two main categories: – an inflectional suffix changes the tense or grammatical status of a word, e.g. from present to past *(worked)* or from singular to plural *(accidents)*; – a derivational suffix changes the word class, e.g. from verb to noun *(worker)* or from noun to adjective *(accidental)*.
summary/summarise	condensing material into a shorter form while still retaining the overall meaning and main points. The written form is sometimes called **précis**. Summarising demonstrates receptive skills of reading or listening comprehension, and evaluation and selection. It also demonstrates productive skills of writing or speaking, in recasting the material concisely and accurately.
syllable/syllabification	each beat in a word is a syllable. Dividing longer words into syllables can help learners understand word structure, which in turn can help reading and spelling.
synonym	a word that has the same meaning (in a particular context) as another word.
syntax	the aspect of grammar that is concerned with the relationship between words, in phrases, clauses and sentences. Language users can make syntactic choices within certain rules and patterns. Adult native speakers have much implicit syntactic knowledge, which can be used to help predict the possible meanings of unknown words within sentences when reading.
technical vocabulary	words that have a particular meaning that depends on the (usually, working) context in which they are used.
tense	a verb form that most often indicates time. English verbs have two basic tenses, present and past, and each of these can be simple or continuous. For example:

present	past
I wait (simple)	*I waited* (simple)
I am waiting (continuous)	*I was waiting* (continuous)

Additionally, all these forms can be perfect (with have):

present perfect	past perfect
I have waited (perfect)	*I had waited* (perfect)
I have been waiting (perfect continuous)	*I had been waiting* (perfect continuous)

English has no specific future tense. Future time can be expressed in a number of ways using will or present tenses. For example: *John will arrive tomorrow; John will be arriving tomorrow; John is going to arrive tomorrow; John is arriving tomorrow; John arrives tomorrow.*

text	words (and images) that are organised to communicate. Includes written, spoken and electronic forms.

turn-taking	one of the most widely recognised conventions of conversation in English-speaking cultures, with people speaking one at a time, taking turns to speak. Speakers develop (consciously or unconsciously) ways of signalling the wish to speak and of indicating to another person that it is their turn.
upper case	a term used to describe capital letters. In print, in any given font and font size, all upper case letters will be the same height.
verb	a word that expresses an action, a happening, a process or a state. It can be thought of as a 'doing' or 'being' word. In the sentence *Mark is tired and wants to go to bed*, *'is'* *'wants'* and *'go'* are verbs. Sometimes two or more words make up a verb phrase, such as *are going, didn't want, has been waiting.*
voice	choice of voice enables the writer or speaker to place the focus on the 'doer' of the action (active voice) or on the action itself and its recipient (passive voice): e.g. *The dog <u>bit</u> Ben. Ben <u>was bitten</u> by the dog.* (See also **active and passive, subject**.)
vowel	a **phoneme** produced without audible friction or closure. Every syllable contains a vowel. A vowel phoneme may be represented by one or more letters. These may be vowels *(m<u>ai</u>d)*, or a combination of vowels and consonants *(st<u>ar</u>t; c<u>ou</u>ld).*
writing frame	a structured prompt to support writing. A writing frame may take the form of opening phrases of paragraphs, and may include suggested vocabulary. It often provides a template for a particular text type.

References

Basic Skills Agency (1999) *Literacy, Leaving School and Jobs: the effect of poor basic skills on employment in different age groups.* London: Basic Skills Agency.

Department for Education and Employment (1998) *The National Literacy Strategy – framework for teaching.* London: DfEE.

Department for Education and Employment (1998) *The National Numeracy Strategy – framework for teaching.* London: DfEE.

Department for Education and Employment (1999) *A Fresh Start – Improving Literacy and Numeracy (The report of the working group chaired by Sir Claus Moser).* London: DfEE.

Department for Education and Employment/Qualifications and Curriculum Authority (2000) *The National Curriculum – handbook for primary teachers in England (key stages 1 and 2).* London: The Stationery Office.

Department for Education and Employment/Qualifications and Curriculum Authority (2000) *The National Curriculum – handbook for secondary teachers in England (key stages 3 and 4).* London: The Stationery Office.

Institute for Employment Studies (1993) *Basic Skills and Jobs.* London: Adult Literacy and Basic Skills Unit.

Qualifications and Curriculum Authority (2000) *National Standards for Adult Literacy and Numeracy.* London: QCA.